DESOLATION OF THE CHIMERA

Luis Cernuda

DESOLATION OF THE CHIMERA

LAST POEMS

Translated by
Stephen Kessler

WHITE PINE PRESS / BUFFALO, NEW YORK

Spanish text taken from the second printing of the fourth edition of *La realidad y el deseo*, published by Fondo de Cultura Económica, Mexico, DF, 1975.

Translation copyright ©2009 by Stephen Kessler

The translator wishes to thank Ángel María Yanguas Cernuda for his patient cooperation and support over the course of this project.

Grateful acknowledgment is also due to the editors of the following periodicals where some of these translations, often in earlier versions, originally appeared: *Basalt, Brindin Press, Calque, Chelsea, Invisible City, Osiris, The Redwood Coast Review, Rhino, Subtropics, Threepenny Review,* and in *Captive Music,* a chapbook from Q Ave Press.

Publication of this book was made possible, in part, by a grant from the National Endowment for the Arts, which believes that a great nation deserves great art, and with public funds from the New York State Council on the Arts, a State Agency.

First Edition.

ISBN: 978-1-935210-00-9

Printed and bound in the United States of America.

Library of Congress Control Number: 2009921873

WHITE PINE PRESS
P.O. Box 236
BUFFALO, NEW YORK 14201

Contents

From *Desolación de la Quimera / Desolation of the Chimera*

Translator's Prologue:
Exile, Eros and the Sublime

Nearing age fifty, in exile for fourteen years from his native Spain—first in Great Britain, then in New England, both uncongenial climates to his Andalusian blood—Luis Cernuda discovered Mexico. The warmth of the air, the sound of his own language, the easy sensuality of the people after the austere reserve of Massachusetts Yankees, combined were too much for the poet to resist. Enamored of a young Mexican man, Cernuda surrendered to the erotic imperative: as soon as possible he quit his teaching job at Mount Holyoke and moved to Mexico.

Born in Seville in 1902, Cernuda gravitated to Madrid in his twenties and, already a promising poet, fell in with the brilliant group of friends that came to be known as the Generation of 1927—fellow Andalusians Pedro Salinas (who had been his professor at the University in Seville), Rafael Alberti, Vicente Aleixandre and Federico García Lorca, the Castilian Jorge Guillén and the Cantabrian Gerardo Diego, among others, including Luis Buñuel and Salvador Dalí. Before long, Cernuda emerged as one of the brightest stars in this constellation. Soon after publication of the first edition of his collected poems, *La realidad y el deseo (Reality and Desire)*, the Civil War began and the golden moment of poetry and friendship was over forever.

The murder of Lorca and the scattering of others into exile or into the mountains to defend the Republic against Francisco Franco's fascist invaders was a cultural cataclysm to match the political and military catastrophe of the next three years—a catastrophe that turned into the protracted nightmare of a four-decades-long dictatorship. In 1938, when things were looking especially bleak in Spain, Cernuda accepted an invitation to lecture in London and never returned. He taught there and in Glasgow, Scotland, until 1947 when he took the position at Mount Holyoke—a women's college where he wouldn't even have the invigorating experience of lusting after his students. Openly homosexual in his life and his writing, Cernuda chronicled his misery during these years of exile in the North even as he continued to create some of his best poems and to establish himself as one of his generation's most astute and respected critics.

Mexico changed his fortunes, and for a while sexual love and the music of the Spanish language restored the poet's spirit. Except for brief academic appointments in the early sixties in California, at San Francisco State and UCLA, he chose a life of poverty in the Mexico City suburb of Coyoacán until his sudden death from a heart attack in 1963. He was sixty-one years old.

This book is a selection from Cernuda's final harvest of verse, published originally in two volumes, *Con las horas contadas (With Time Running Out)* and *Desolación de la Quimera.* The poems date from 1950 to 1962 and show a master at work with nothing left to prove. Cut off from his country and from his native audience, he writes as if for himself alone, with little hope that his work will find future readers. Embittered by exile and despairing of his sorry fate, he is ironically unaware that his poetry is increasingly coming to be seen by younger Spaniards as representative of the best of his generation. In the intervening years his stature has only risen. His rootlessness, his alienation, his marginality as a gay man, his cosmopolitan perspective and his estheticism all resonated with the new generations coming of age in Spain under dictatorship, and even more so in the cultural opening since Franco's death in 1975.

The poems Cernuda wrote during the last dozen years of his life display not only his unbroken devotion to poetry, nor just the anger and gloom of a man denied the fulfillment he felt he had earned through his unswerving commitment to the beautiful, but a sustained engagement with beauty and pleasure—or the memory of pleasure—as well as with the immortal monuments of literature, art and music. The lives and works of El Greco, Mozart, Keats, Titian, Ruskin, and other masters are invoked as measures of humanity's potential despite the bad faith, cruelties and pettiness of politics, war and commerce. Cernuda identifies with an artistic aristocracy, a kind of secular priesthood, whose vocation and duty it is to nourish the human soul and give life meaning. He reimagines the lives of sensitive kings—Philip II of Spain and Louis II of Bavaria, to name two—never suited to the vulgar demands of ruling. He sympathizes with the plight of these historic misfits whose tragic failures and dissatisfactions mirror his own.

Yet despite the despair of exile and the urgent sense of his own impending doom—as the book title indicates, even in his fifties he could feel his time running out—Cernuda's muse somehow kept him connected to the consolations of nostalgia, the bittersweet memory of happier times in the Andalucía of his youth and in the brief embrace of his Mexican paramour, who ultimately abandoned him. The poems invoking the little plazas and orange blossoms of Seville and what Blake called "the lineaments of gratified desire" rescue the poet from abject hopelessness and bring back, in durable form, the afterimages of ephemeral pleasures. Sensory, spiritual and emotional bliss is partially recovered in the lyric lines of the aging writer's verse. His life, bitter as it feels to him, salvages by way of poetry a redeeming sweetness to be savored long after, first by the writer and eventually by others.

These late poems of Cernuda have until now been largely neglected by North American translators, and so are unknown to most readers of English. The neglect can be explained in part by the classical tenor of his voice and the somewhat lofty formality of his diction—the opposite of the ironic, kinetic, hip and colloquial mannerism that supposedly sounds most "natural" to the contemporary American ear. Yet Cernuda was out of step with his own contemporaries as well, and his direct style was nearly as untimely then.

What I have tried to do as a translator is to honor the original tone of Cernuda's poems while bringing his lyric voice into as speakable a modern American idiom as possible. I have sought to sustain the tension between his high esthetic ideals and the lived reality of his experience, which might be that of any aging artist who feels he has lost the most vital years of his life stranded in unfriendly circumstances and in pursuit of an unattainable measure of perfection—an artist who, to make matters worse, has failed to attract the attention he'd hoped for when he first embarked on the creative path.

Cernuda's biographical trajectory, and a lyric-philosophical history of his sensibility, can be traced in his collected prose poems, *Written in Water*, which City Lights published in my translation in 2004. His *Selected Poems*, translated by Reginald Gibbons, was reissued in paperback by Sheep Meadow Press in 2000. This volume supplements those and begins to bring to light in English a more substantial yet still relatively slim fragment of the work of one of the twentieth century's most important Spanish-language poets.

The critic Harold Bloom, in his book *Genius*, calls Cernuda a "saint" of the art of poetry, comparing him in this aspect to Emily Dickinson and Paul Celan. García Lorca famously complained, shortly before his death in 1936, that Cernuda's poems set a maddening standard of perfection, of sublimity. For the twenty-first century reader the sublime may seem an archaic idea, but my hope in this book is to recover Cernuda's sense of poetic possibility: that poetry at its best is able not only to record the growth and the existential truth of a proud soul but also to evoke the archetypal forms of timeless inspiration—and their inherent danger—the joyful turmoil and destructive power of a paradoxically chimerical yet authentic vision of poetic creation. Cernuda served that vision his whole life, and my goal as a translator has been to serve his with something approaching his own fidelity.

—Stephen Kessler

From

Con las horas contadas

With Time Running Out

[1950–1956]

La poesía

Para tu siervo el sino le escogiera,
Y absorto y entregado, el niño
¿Qué podía hacer sino seguirte?

El mozo luego, enamorado, conocía
Tu poder sobre él, y lo ha servido
Como a nada en la vida, contra todo.

Pero el hombre algún día, al preguntarse:
La servidumbre larga qué le ha deparado,
Su libertad envidió a uno, a otro su fortuna.

Y quiso ser él mismo, no servirte
Más, y vivir para sí, entre los hombres.
Tú le dejaste, como a un niño, a su capricho.

Pero después, pobre sin ti de todo,
A tu voz que llamaba, o al sueño de ella,
Vivo en su servidumbre respondió: "Señora".

Poetry

Chosen by fate to be your servant, and
Consumed and given over as he was,
What choice did the boy have but to follow?

Later in love the young man understood
Your power over him, and submitted to it
Against everything, as to nothing else in life.

But one day when the grown man asked himself
What he had gained from this long servitude,
He envied one man his freedom, another his fortune.

And he tried to be just himself, and not serve you
Anymore, and live for himself, among other men.
You left him, like a child, to his caprice.

But later, bereft of everything without you,
When he heard your call, or dreamed it,
Ever your servant, he replied, "My Lady."

Retrato de poeta

(Fray H. F. Paravicino, por El Greco)

A Ramón Gaya

¿También tú aquí, hermano, amigo,
Maestro, en este limbo? ¿Quién te trajo,
Locura de los nuestros, que es la nuestra,
Como a mí? ¿O codicia, vendiendo el patrimonio
No ganado, sino heredado, de aquellos que no saben
Quererlo? Tú no puedes hablarme, y yo apenas
Si puedo hablar. Mas tus ojos me miran
Como si a ver un pensamiento me llamaran.

Y pienso. Estás mirando allá. Asistes
Al tiempo aquel parado, a lo que era
En el momento aquel, cuando el pintor termina
Y te deja mirando quietamente tu mundo
A la ventana: aquel paisaje bronco
De rocas y de encinas, verde todo y moreno,
En azul contrastado a la distancia,
De un contorno tan neto que parece triste.

Aquella tierra estás mirando, la ciudad aquella,
La gente aquella. El brillante revuelo
Miras de terciopelo y seda, de metales
Y esmaltes, de plumajes y blondas,
Con su estremecimiento, su palpitar humano
Que agita el aire como ala enloquecida
De mediodía. Por eso tu mirada
Está mirando así, nostálgica, indulgente.

Portrait of a Poet

(Brother H. F. Paravicino, by El Greco)

for Ramón Gaya

You too here in this limbo, brother,
Friend, teacher? Who brought you,
Our people's madness, ours, as it did me?
Or greed, our patrimony unearned but inherited,
Sold off by those who never learned to love it.
You can't answer me, and I can barely speak,
If even that. But your eyes meet mine
As if they were calling me to see a thought.

And I'm thinking. You're there looking. You're present
In that stopped time, in what was
That moment, when the painter is done
And leaves you gazing quietly out the window
At your world: that rugged landscape
Of rocks and hills, all green and brown,
Contrasted against a distant blue,
So clear in outline that it seems sad.

You're looking out at that land, that city,
Those people. You see the shiny
Stirrings of silk and velvet, of metals,
Enamels, feathers and lace,
With their shimmerings, their human heartbeat
Rippling the air like a maddened wing
At noon. That's why your gaze
Is watching that way, nostalgic, indulgent.

El instinto te dice que ese vivir soberbio
Levanta la palabra. La palabra es más plena
Ahí, más rica, y fulge igual que otros joyeles,
Otras espadas, al cruzar sus destellos y sus filos
En el campo teñido de poniente y de sangre,
En la noche encendida, al compás del sarao
O del rezo en la nave. Esa palabra, de la cual tú conoces,
Por el verso y la plática, su poder y su hechizo.

Esa palabra de ti amada, sometiendo
A la encumbrada muchedumbre, le recuerda
Cómo va nuestra fe hacia las cosas
Ya no vistas afuera con los ojos,
Aunque dentro las ven tan claras nuestras almas;
Las cosas mismas que sostienen tu vida,
Como la tierra aquella, sus encinas, sus rocas,
Que estás ahí mirando quietamente.

Yo no las veo ya, y apenas si ahora escucho,
Gracias a ti, su dejo adormecido
Queriendo resurgir, buscando el aire
Otra vez. En los nidos de antaño
No hay pájaros, amigo. Ahí perdona y comprende;
Tan caídos estamos que ni la fe nos queda.
Me miras, y tus labios, con pausa reflexiva,
Devoran silenciosos las palabras amargas.

Instinct tells you that language arises
From that magnificent life. Language is fuller
There, richer, and shines like those other jewels,
Those other swords, their flashing edges crossing
In the sunset- and blood-stained countryside,
In the lit-up night, in the courtyard soirée
Or at prayer in the nave. That language, which you know well,
Through poetry and talk, its power and the spell it casts.

That language, loved by you, looking out
On the lofty crowd, is a reminder of
What happens to our faith toward things
Unseen by our eyes outside,
Though inside, our souls can see so clearly;
The very things that keep you alive,
Like that land, its hills, its rocks,
Which you're there looking out on without a word.

I can no longer see them, but thanks to you
I can just barely hear what's left of them,
Asleep but trying to rise, coming up for air
Again. There are no birds left
In yesterday's nests, old friend. Forgive and understand;
We've fallen so far, not even faith is left us.
You look at me, your lips pause to reflect,
Quietly taking in these bitter words.

Dime. Dime. No esas cosas amargas, las sutiles,
Hondas, afectuosas, que mi oído
Jamás escucha. Como concha vacía,
Mi oído guarda largamente la nostalgia
De su mundo extinguido. Yo aquí solo,
Aun más que lo estás tú, mi hermano y mi maestro,
Mi ausencia en esa tuya busca acorde,
Como ola en la ola. Dime, amigo.

¿Recuerdas? ¿En qué miedos el acento
Armonioso habéis dejado? ¿Lo recuerdas?
Aquel pájaro tuyo adolecía
De esta misma pasión que aquí me trae
Frente a ti. Y aunque yo estoy atado
A prisión menos pía que la suya,
Aún me solicita el viento, el viento
Nuestro, que animó nuestras palabras.

Amigo, amigo, no me hablas. Quietamente
Sentado ahí, en dejadez airosa,
La mano delicada marcando con un dedo
El pasaje en el libro, erguido como a escucha
Del coloquio un momento interrumpido,
Miras tu mundo y en tu mundo vives.
Tú no sufres ausencia, no la sientes;
Pero por ti y por mí sintiendo, la deploro.

Tell me. Tell me. Not those bitter things, but the subtle,
Deep, affectionate ones my ears
Never hear anymore. Like an empty shell,
My ear holds a long nostalgia
For its dead world. Here all alone,
Even more than you are, brother and teacher,
My absence looks for a harmony in yours,
As one wave in another. Speak to me, friend.

Remember? What kinds of fears caused you to lose
Your beautiful accent? Remember?
That bird of yours suffered
From the same passion that brings me here
To face you. And though I'm bound
In a prison less pious than his,
That wind still calls me, our wind,
Which brought our language to life.

Friend, old friend, you're not talking. Quietly
Sitting there, in graceful laziness,
Your delicate hand marking your place
In the book with a finger, alert as if listening
To a conversation that's been briefly interrupted,
You look at your world and live in your world.
Absence is not a source of pain for you;
But I grieve over it, feeling it for us both.

El norte nos devora, presos en esta tierra,
La fortaleza del fastidio atareado,
Por donde sólo van sombras de hombres,
Y entre ellas mi sombra, aunque ésta en ocio,
Y en su ocio conoce más la burla amarga
De nuestra suerte. Tú viviste tu día,
Y en él, con otra vida que el pintor te infunde,
Existes hoy. Yo ¿estoy viviendo el mío?

¿Yo? El instrumento dulce y animado,
Un eco aquí de las tristezas nuestras.

The north consumes us, prisoners in this land,
Fortress of overworked annoyances,
Where only shadows of men exist,
And my shadow among them, even though idle,
And in its idleness it understands the bitter joke
Of our fate. You lived your day,
And in it, with this other life the painter gives you,
You exist today. And me, am I living mine?

Me? I'm just a high-strung instrument,
An echo here of all our sadnesses.

Instrumento músico

Si para despertar las notas,
Con una pluma de águila
Pulsaba el músico árabe
Las cuerdas del laúd,

Para despertar la palabra,
¿La pluma de qué ave
Pulsada por qué mano
Es la que hiere en ti?

Musical Instrument

If the Arab musician
Plucks the lute strings
With an eagle quill
To awaken the notes,

What hand plucks
With what bird's quill
The wound in you
That awakens the word?

Nocturno yanqui

La lámpara y la cortina
Al pueblo en su sombra excluyen.
Sueña ahora,
Si puedes, si te contentas
Con sueños, cuando te faltan
Realidades.

Estás aquí, de regreso
Del mundo, ayer vivo, hoy
Cuerpo en pena,
Esperando locamente,
Alrededor tuyo, amigos
Y sus voces.

Callas y escuchas. No. Nada
Oyes, excepto tu sangre,
Su latido
Incansable, temeroso;
Y atención prestas a otra
Cosa inquieta.

Es la madera, que cruje;
Es el radiador, que silba.
Un bostezo.
Pausa. Y el reloj consultas:
Todavía temprano para
Acostarte.

Yankee Nocturne

The lamp and curtain
Shut out the darkened town.
Dream now,
If you can, if you can be happy
With dreams, when reality's
Wanting.

You're here, returned
From the world, alive yesterday, today
A miserable body
Madly wishing
For friends and their voices
Around you.

Quiet, you listen. No. You hear
Nothing but your blood,
Its tireless
Fearful pulse;
And you notice another
Unquiet thing.

It's the wood, creaking;
It's the radiator, whistling.
A yawn.
A pause. You check the clock:
Still too early
For bed.

Tomas un libro. Mas piensas
Que has leído demasiado
Con los ojos,
Y a tus años la lectura
Mejor es recuerdo de unos
Libros viejos,
Pero con nuevo sentido.

¿Qué hacer? Porque tiempo hay.
Es temprano.
Todo el invierno te espera,
Y la primavera entonces.
Tiempo tienes.

¿Mucho? ¿Cuánto? ¿Y hasta cuándo
El tiempo al hombre le dura?
"No, que es tarde,
Es tarde", repite alguno
Dentro de ti, que no eres.
Y suspiras.

La vida en tiempo se vive,
Tu eternidad es ahora,
Porque luego
No habrá tiempo para nada
Tuyo. Gana tiempo. ¿Y cuándo?

You pick up a book. But you think
You've read too much
With those eyes,
And at your age the best
Reading is the memory of a few
Old books,
But with new meaning.

What to do? Because there's still time.
It's early.
The whole winter's ahead of you,
And then spring.
You have time.

A lot? How much? And how long
Does time really last a man?
"No, it's late,
It's late," someone repeats
Inside you, who isn't you.
You take a breath.

Life is lived in time,
And your eternity is now,
Because later
There'll be no time for anything
Of yours. Time wins. And how much longer?

Alguien dijo:
"El tiempo y yo para otros
Dos". ¿Cuáles dos? ¿Dos lectores
De mañana?
Mas tus lectores, si nacen,
Y tu tiempo, no coinciden.
Estás solo
Frente al tiempo, con tu vida
Sin vivir.

     Remordimiento.
Fuiste joven,
Pero nunca lo supiste
Hasta hoy, que el ave ha huido
De tu mano.

La mocedad dentro duele,
Tú su presa vengadora,
Conociendo
Que, pues no le va esta cara
Ni el pelo blanco, es inútil
Por tardía.

El trabajo alivia a otros
De lo que no tiene cura,
Según dicen.
¿Cuántos años ahora tienes
De trabajo? ¿Veinte y pico
Mal contados?

Someone once said:
"Time and I for two
Others." Which two?
Two readers
Tomorrow?
But your readers, if any, ever,
And your time don't coincide.
You're alone
Up against time, with your life
Unlived.

     Remorse, regret.
You were young,
But till now you never knew
The bird had flown
From your hand.

The youth inside you aches,
You are its angry prey,
Knowing
That since this face and this white hair
Aren't going anywhere, it's pointless
And too late.

To others, work is some relief
For what has no cure,
Or so they say.
How many years have you been
Working now? Twenty and counting
Ill accounted for?

Trabajo fue que no compra
Para ti la independencia
Relativa.
A otro menester el mundo,
Generoso como siempre,
Te demanda.

Y profesas pues, ganando
Tu vida, no con esfuerzo,
Con fastidio.
Nadie enseña lo que importa,
Que eso ha de aprenderlo el hombre
Por sí solo.

Lo mejor que has sido, diste,
Lo mejor de tu existencia,
A una sombra:
Al afán de hacerte digno,
Al deseo de excederte,
Esperando
Siempre mañana otro día
Que, aunque tarde, justifique
Tu pretexto.

Cierto que tú te esforzaste
Por sino y amor de una
Criatura,
Mito moceril, buscando
Desde siempre, y al servirla,
Ser quien eres.

Work that never purchased
For you the slightest
Independence.
Generous as ever, the world
Demands of you
Another kind of work.

And you take your vows, earning
Your living not by effort
But by aggravation.
Nobody teaches what's important,
Everyone has to learn that
For himself.

The best that you've been,
The best part of your existence
Given to a shadow:
The zeal to be worthy,
Desire to excel,
Always waiting
For a new day tomorrow
When, even belatedly, your purpose
Would be justified.

It's true you made an effort
For destiny and for someone's
Love,
The myth of youth, forever
In search of it, and serving it,
To be who you are.

Y al que eras le has hallado.
¿Mas es la verdad del hombre
Para él solo,
Como un inútil secreto?
¿Por qué no poner la vida
A otra cosa?

Quien eres, tu vida era;
Uno sin otro no sois,
Tú lo sabes.
Y es fuerza seguir, entonces,
Aun el miraje perdido,
Hasta el día
Que la historia se termine,
Para ti al menos.

    Y piensas
Que así vuelves
Donde estabas al comienzo
Del soliloquio: contigo
Y sin nadie.

Mata la luz, y a la cama.

And you've found who you were.
But is a man's truth
For him alone,
Like a useless secret?
Why not apply one's life
To something else?

Whoever you are, your life was;
You know you can't be one
Without the other.
And it takes strength to go on, then,
With no illusions,
Until the day
When the story ends,
At least for you.

      And you think
That's how you come back
To where you started
The soliloquy: by yourself
And with no one.

Out with the light, and go to bed.

Palabra amada

—¿Qué palabra es la que más te gusta?
—¿Una palabra? ¿Tan sólo una?
¿Y quién responde a esa pregunta?

—¿La prefieres por su sonido?
—Por lo callado de su ritmo,
Que deja un eco cuando se ha dicho.

—¿O la prefieres por lo que expresa?
—Por todo lo que en ella tiembla,
Hiriendo el pecho como saeta.

—Esa palabra dímela tú.
—Esa palabra es: andaluz.

Best Loved Word

"What word is it that pleases you the most?"
"One word, only one?
And who is it answering such a question?"

"Do you love it for its sound?"
"For the quietness of its rhythm,
Which leaves an echo after it's spoken."

"Or do you love it for what it says?"
"For everything trembling in it,
Piercing my chest like a dart."

"What word is it, tell me the truth."
"The word is: *andaluz.*"

Limbo

A Octavio Paz

La plaza sola (gris el aire,
Negros los árboles, la tierra
Manchada por la nieve),
Parecía, no realidad, mas copia
Triste sin realidad. Entonces,
Ante el umbral, dijiste:
Viviendo aquí serías
Fantasma de ti mismo.

Inhóspita en su adorno
Parsimonioso, porcelanas, bronces,
Muebles chinos, la casa
Oscura toda era,
Pálidas sus ventanas sobre el río,
Y el color se escondía
En un retablo español, en un lienzo
Francés, su brío amedrentado.

Entre aquellos despojos,
Provecto, el dueño estaba
Sentando junto a su retrato
Por artista a la moda en años idos,
Imagen fatua y fácil
Del *dilettante*, divertido entonces
Comprando lo que una fe creara
En otro tiempo y otra tierra.

Limbo

for Octavio Paz

The empty square (gray air,
Black trees, the ground
Spotted with snow)
Appeared to be not reality but a sad
Unreal copy. Then,
At the threshold, you said:
Living here you'd be
A ghost of yourself.

Inhospitable in its dull
Decor, porcelains, bronzes,
Chinese furniture, the house
Was dark inside,
Its windows pale above the river,
And the only color hidden
In a Spanish altarpiece, on a French
Canvas, its energy terrifying.

Amid those spoils,
Provided for, the owner was
Seated beside his portrait
Done by an artist in vogue some years ago,
The fatuous, facile image
Of a dilettante, amused then
To purchase what a faith had created
In another time and land.

Allí con sus iguales,
Damas imperativas bajo sus afeites,
Caballeros seguros de sí mismos,
Rito social cumplía,
Y entre el diálogo moroso,
Tú oyendo alguien que dijo: "Me ofrecieron
La primera edición de un poeta raro,
Y la he comprado", tu emoción callaste.

Así, pensabas, el poeta
Vive para esto, para esto
Noches y días amargos, sin ayuda
De nadie, en la contienda
Adonde, como el fénix, muere y nace,
Para que años después, siglos
Después, obtenga al fin el displicente
Favor de un grande en este mundo.

Su vida ya puede excusarse,
Porque ha muerto del todo;
Su trabajo ahora cuenta,
Domesticado para el mundo de ellos,
Como otro objeto vano,
Otro ornamento inútil;
Y tú cobarde, mudo
Te despediste ahí, como el que asiente,
Más allá de la muerte, a la injusticia.

Mejor la destrucción, el fuego.

There among his peers,
Imperious ladies behind their makeup,
Gentlemen sure of themselves,
He played his role in the ritual,
And somewhere in the turgid conversation
Hearing someone say, "I was offered
The first edition of a rare poet,
And I bought it," you couldn't speak what you felt.

So the poet lives
For this, you thought, for this
The bitter nights and days, with no one's
Help, in the contest
Where, like a phoenix, he dies and is born
So that years later, centuries
Later, he may at last obtain the offhand
Favor of some self-important person in this world.

His life can now be excused,
Because he's died for good;
Domesticated to suit their world,
His work now counts
As one more bauble,
One more useless accessory.
And cowardly you, without a word,
Excused yourself and left, as one who accepts
Injustice beyond the grave.

Better the work should be destroyed, or burned.

Nochebuena cincuenta y una

Amor, dios oscuro,
Que a nosotros viene
Otra vez, probando
Su esperanza siempre.

Ha nacido. El frío,
La sombra, la muerte,
Todo el desamparo
Humano es su suerte.

Desamparo humano
Que el amor no puede
Ayudar. ¿Podría
Él, cuando tan débil

Contra nuestro engaño
Su fuerza se vuelve,
Siendo sólo aliento
De bestia inocente?

Velad pues, pastores;
Adorad pues, reyes,
Su sueño amoroso
Que el mundo escarnece.

Christmas Eve Fifty-one

Love, the dark god
Who comes to us
Again, testing
His hope as always.

He's born. The cold,
Darkness, death,
All human home-
Lessness his fate.

Human homelessness
Which love can't
Help. Could he,
When his strength

Goes weak
Against our deception,
Being only a breath
Of an innocent beast?

So stay awake, shepherds;
Worship, kings,
His dream of love
The world derides.

Águila y rosa

Lo que el bisabuelo sembrara, el padre quiere cosecharlo,
Y para su codicia de coronas, ocasión es esta
De añadir una más. En su rincón, Castilla nada dice,
Mas paga, como siempre, con dinero, con sudor, con sangre.
Una vez protestó. ¿Y ahora? De nuevo va al tablero su destino.

Cuando el príncipe toca puerto en Inglaterra, es el verano.
El cielo envía entonces alguna luz sobre la isla,
Regocijando tierra adentro tantos prados morosos,
Y a la sangre invernal la despierta y provoca.
Aunque sólo dure unos días, la luz parece eterna.

Dura tarea es, y fastidiosa, la del poder, caído
En sus manos tan mozas todavía, y sin costumbre
De la tierra y la gente, que acaso no le quieran y recelen,
Pero sobre la cual debe reinar, bajo la cual debe doblegarse,
Postergando el ser propio y sus modos de España.

Festivos trajes toda, mas semblantes nublados,
La muchedumbre está en el puerto, y le mira
Entre curiosa y enemiga, como al que viene de otro mundo.
Ésa debe regir. Su voluntad es grande y está pronta
A la llamada del destino, frente a la cual no hay vuelta.

Pendones y estandartes le saludan, y el mozo, a quien dotara
Tan bien naturaleza en apariencia y pensamiento,
Un poco en su reserva cede y en su distancia otro,
Para hallar el latido de aquellas criaturas,
Aunque todo parece, allá en su mente, remoto, inabordable.

Eagle and Rose

What the great-grandfather sowed, the father wants to reap,
And in his greed for crowns, this is the chance
To add one more. In its corner, Castile says nothing,
But pays, as always, with treasure and sweat and blood.
At one time it protested. But now? Again its destiny is on the table.

It's summer when the prince sets foot in England.
The sky spreads a certain light over the island,
So many sluggish meadows dancing for joy,
The wintry blood awakened and provoked.
Though it lasts just a few days, the light seems eternal.

The work of power is hard and tedious, fallen
Into his hands that are still so young, and unfamiliar
With this land and people, who may not like him, who distrust him,
But over whom he must reign, and before whom he must bend,
Deferring his own being and his Spanish ways.

Everyone festively dressed, but looking gloomy,
The crowd is in the harbor, peering at him
Part curious, part hostile, as if he were coming from another world.
He's the one who must rule. His will is strong and ready
For destiny's call, from which there's no turning back.

Banners and flags salute him, and the youth, gifted
With such good looks and a bright mind,
Gives up a bit of his reserve and some of his distance
In order to feel the pulse of those strange people,
Though everything seems to him remote and unapproachable.

Ella en su camarín espera, casi marchito el cuerpo,
Dentro del cual la adolescencia no vivida tiembla
De deseo y angustia, las galas suntuosas subrayando
El empaque monástico, en los labios la difícil sonrisa,
En la mano esa rosa, esa esperanza del amor tardío.

Si a la herencia paterna, densa de infamia y crimen,
La materna rescata, limpia en el sufrimiento silencioso,
Tras los años de escarnio, su Dios quizá le debe
Un pedazo de dicha, algo que alivie el dejo amargo
De la vida, aunque sea ahora, cuando la mocedad se ha ido.

Repican las campanas y vibran las trompetas,
Todo el aire está lleno de un rojo son metálico,
Como alfombra del príncipe. Encima el cielo abre
Su más pomposo azul, sus nubes más marmóreas.
Ella supo esperar, desesperando, la llegada.

¿No es la voz del arcángel ese clamor que oye,
Como salutación del hijo que ha de encarnar su vientre?
En el dintel está. Por sus ojos nublados entra la imagen:
Negra figura airosa, relámpago dorado del cabello,
Azul de unas pupilas que a las suyas se cruzan.

Mas la gala del mundo no es la fiesta del cielo,
Y con ceño nublado amanece a las bodas,
Aunque azul está en ella, y brilla en diamantes
Sobre la seda alba, y templa en voces puras.
Postrados ante Dios, María y Felipe son uno en la carne.

She waits in her dressing room, her body almost withered,
Holding its unlived adolescence trembling
With anguish and desire, the sumptuous gown accentuating
Her monastic look, a forced smile on her lips,
In her hand that rose, that hope for belated love.

If the father's legacy, thick with infamy and crime,
Is redeemed by the mother's, pure in its silent suffering,
Across years of mockery, her God perhaps owes her
A bit of happiness, something to relieve the bitter taste
Of life, even now, when her youth has fled.

The bells are rung and the trumpets blown,
The air is filled with a metallic sound, red
As a prince's carpet. Overhead the sky opens
Its most glorious blue, its most marbly clouds.
She knew how to wait, without hope, for his arrival.

Is the noise she hears not the voice of the archangel,
Like a greeting for the child to be formed in her womb?
She stands at the window. Into her hooded eyes comes the image:
A dark and graceful figure, his hair a flash of gold lightning,
Blue of two eyes that meet hers.

But the earth's feast is not heaven's festival,
And the wedding day dawns with a cloudy frown,
Even though there is blue in it, and glittering diamonds
Over the silken dawn, and it warms into pure voices.
Kneeling before God, Mary and Philip are joined in flesh.

Ama Felipe la calma, la quietud contemplativa;
Si un mundo bello hay fuera, otro más bello hay dentro.
Quiere vivir en ambos, pero estos seres sólo
Viven afuera, y el ocio fértil de la mente les aburre.
Por eso él debe ahora hacer jornada activa y practicar deportes.

Cuan bien lo disimula su aburrimiento. Habla, bebe, juega.
Domesticado creen al tan soberbio mozo. Mas sabe el sutil modo
De servir cuando manda, de exaltarse cuando así se humilla,
Y de su entraña a veces vienen dichos preñados de futuro:
"Prefiero no reinar, a reinar sobre heréticos".

Aunque vencido su disgusto es afable o lo parece,
Y dice blandamente, cuando uno temeroso se le acerca, "Sosegaos",
No se lo perdonaron, no le perdonan nunca
Este miedo que en su presencia les doblaba.
Aún por eso le odian, odiando ahí aquella imagen de sí mismos.

Así murmuran de él. Así le envidian. Y con rabia
Denigran su grandeza, que no sabe prestarse
A los prácticos modos de engañar la conciencia,
A la nación de hormigas la tierra socavando,
Al pueblo de tenderos acumulando, y no siempre lo propio.

Ella gobierna y calla; ama y en el hijo confía,
Como aguardó al esposo, aguardándole ahora,
Y al creerle llegado el gozo la hace joven.
Pero todo fue engaño; rezó y esperó en vano.
Y con el hijo ve escapar al esposo juntamente.

Philip loves calm, contemplative quietude;
If the world outside is lovely, the one within is lovelier.
He'd like to live in both, but these beings only
Live outwardly, and the fertile idleness of the mind bores them.
That's why he has to fill his days with activities and sports.

How well he hides his boredom. He talks, he drinks, he plays.
They think the proud young man has been domesticated. But he knows the
                    subtle way
To serve while he commands, to exalt and humble himself at the same time,
And out of his depths at times come sayings heavy with the future:
"I'd rather not reign than reign over heretics."

Though he appears to have conquered his distaste and seems to be friendly,
And softly says, when someone timidly approaches him, "Be calm,"
They don't forgive him, they never forgive him
For this fear that in his presence bows them down.
Even for this they hate him, hating the very image of themselves.

So they gossip about him. They envy him. And viciously
Denigrate his greatness, which knows nothing of how to apply itself
To the practical methods of tricking his conscience,
To a nation of ants digging tunnels in the earth,
Of shopkeepers accumulating, and not always what's theirs.

She governs and is silent; she loves and trusts in her child,
As she protected her husband, protecting him now,
And believing him arrived the joy makes her feel young.
But it was all a trick; she prayed and waited in vain.
And she watches husband and child escape together.

49

El mozo castellano, lejos de cuanto es suyo,
Haciendo de marido junto a la reina estéril,
Junto a un pueblo relapso de monarca católico,
Mira a sus españoles, pero nada les dice.
"Sácame de aquí, ay, Dios de mi tierra", canta un día un soldado.

Ya la pausa es bien larga, y la impaciencia es grande.
Su alma no está aquí, sino donde ha nacido.
Su centro está en su tierra, su hogar, al que será tan dulce
Cuidarlo, dirigirlo. Ni el mismo amor podría
Acaso retenerle. Y a esta mujer ¿la ama?

No son los nuestros afectos ni tareas
Si en tierra que no es nuestra los hallamos.
¿Pudo sino marcharse? Su mano juntos tuvo
En la pausa imposible, como en la del poniente
Luz y sombra, el cetro contrario de dos pueblos.

Ya no le queda a ella sino morir a solas,
Sin hijo y sin esposo, mirando el cielo bajo
Que pesa como losa anticipada. Pero su vida ha conocido,
Si no la flor, su sombra; entonces no fue estéril,
Y valía la pena de vivirse, con toda esa amargura.

Y a él, hacer que el mundo escuche y siga
La pauta de la fe. Pudo mover los hombres,
Hasta donde terminan los designios humanos
Y empiezan los divinos. Ahí su voluntad descansa.
Con ese acatamiento reina y muere y vive.

The young Castilian, far from everything that's his,
Playing at being husband to the barren queen,
Next to a population lapsed from a Catholic monarch,
Looks at his Spaniards but doesn't say a word.
"Get me out of here, oh God of my land," a soldier cries one day.

The interval has lasted a long while, and he's getting impatient.
His soul isn't here but where it was born.
His center is in his land, his home, it would be so sweet
To manage, take care of it. Not even love could
Likely keep him here. And does he love this woman?

Our affections and our works are no longer ours
If we find ourselves in a land that isn't ours.
What could he do but leave? He held in his hand,
In the impossible interval, as in the sunset's lingering
Light and darkness, rule over two completely different peoples.

Nothing is left for her but to die alone,
With neither child nor husband, watching the low sky
Weighing on her like a gravestone. Yet her life has known,
If not the flower, its shadow; then she wasn't barren,
And living was worthwhile, even with all that bitterness.

And for him it's left to make the world listen and follow
The lines of faith. He could move men,
Up to where human plans end
And the divine begin. That's where his will settles.
Obeying that call he reigns and dies and lives.

In memoriam A. G.

Con él su vida entera coincidía,
Toda promesa y realidad iguales,
La mocedad austera vuelta apenas
Gozosa madurez, tan demoradas
Como día estival. Así olvidaste,
Amando su existir, temer su muerte.

Pero su muerte, al allegarle ahora,
Calló la voz que cerca nunca oíste,
A cuyos ecos despertaron tantos
Sueños del mundo en ti nunca vividos,
Hoy no soñados porque ya son vida.

Cuando para seguir nos falta aliento,
Roto el mágico encanto de las cosas,
Si en soledad alzabas la cabeza,
Sonreír le veías tras sus libros.
Ya entre ellos y tú falta su sombra,
Falta su sombra noble ya en la vida.

Usándonos a ciegas todo sigue,
Aunque unos pocos, como tú, os digáis:
Lo que con él termina en nuestro mundo
No volverá a este mundo. Y no hay consuelo,
Que el tiempo es duro y sin virtud los hombres.
Bien pocos seres que admirar te quedan.

In Memoriam A. G.

He and his life were in perfect time,
Reality measuring up to every promise,
Austere young manhood turned just so
To full maturity, slow
As a summer day. And that's how,
Loving his life, you neglected to fear his death.

And yet his death, arriving for him now,
Has silenced the voice you never heard up close,
Whose echoes awakened so many
Dreams of a world where you never lived,
And now not dreamed because they are life itself.

When you were out of breath to keep on going,
The magic spell of everything now broken,
If in your solitude you raised your head,
You could still see him smiling through his books.
Now between them and you his shadow is missing,
Now his elegant shadow is gone from life.

Everything goes on blindly using us up,
Though a few, like you, may say to yourselves:
What comes to an end in our world with him
Won't come back to this world. And there's no consolation,
Since time is hard and men are good for nothing.
So very few beings are left for you to admire.

El viajero

Eres tú quien respira
Este cálido aire
Nocturno, entre las hojas
Perennes. ¿No te extraña

Ir así, en el halago
De otro clima? Parece
Maravilla imposible
Estar tan libre. Mira

Desde una palma oscura
Gotear las estrellas.
Lo que ves ¿es tu sueño
O tu verdad? El mundo

Mágico que llevabas
Dentro de ti, esperando
Tan largamente, afuera
Surge a la luz. Si ahora

Tu sueño al fin coincide
Con tu verdad, no pienses
Que esta verdad es frágil,
Más aún que aquel sueño.

The Traveler

It's you who's breathing
This warm night air
Among the unfalling
Leaves. Isn't it strange

Slipping like this into the pleasure
Of another climate? It seems
An impossible marvel
To be so free. Look

From under a dark palm
Up at the dripping stars.
Is what you're seeing a dream
Or is it true? The magical

World you carried
Within, waited
So long for, flares
Into light outside. If now

Your dream is at last aligned
With your truth, don't think
This truth is any more
Fragile than that dream.

Otra fecha

Aires claros, nopal y palma,
En los alrededores, saben,
Si no igual, casi igual a como
La tierra tuya aquella antes.

También tú igual me pareces,
O casi igual, al que antes eras:
En el casi sólo consiste,
De ayer a hoy, la diferencia.

En tu hoy más que precario
Nada anterior echas de menos,
Porque lo ido está bien ido,
Como lo muerto está bien muerto.

El futuro, a pesar de todo,
Usa un señuelo que te engaña:
El sí y el no de azar no usado,
El no sé qué donde algo aguarda.

Tú lo sabes, aunque tan tibio
Es tu vivir entre la gente,
Pues si nada crees, aun queriendo,
Aun sin querer crees a veces.

Another Day

Clear air, nopal and palm,
Surrounding you, must know,
If not the same, almost the same
Land as your own before.

You seem the same to me too,
Or almost the same, as before:
The difference from then to now
Consists in the almost alone.

In your more than uncertain today
You miss nothing from before,
For what's gone is truly gone,
As what's dead is truly dead.

The future, in spite of everything,
Uses a bait that fools you:
The yes and the no of chances not taken,
The who knows what where something awaits.

You know it, although your life
Is lukewarm around other people,
And you believe nothing, yet wanting to,
Though sometimes not even wanting to, you believe.

Un momento todavía

Grisáceo el mar y verde;
El aire, igual, lo envuelve.
Dios en su cielo llueve.

Por la rama del pino
Japonés, brota un trino:
Pájaro ya en su nido.

Entra; es tarde. Las olas,
Creciendo con las sombras,
Lentas la playa borran.

En la ventana abierta
De la casa, aún te quedas
Sin saber lo que esperas.

A Moment Held Still

The sea a grayish green,
Wrapped in the same sky.
God in his heaven rains.

On the branch of the Japanese
Pine, a trill is heard:
A bird in its nest.

Go in; it's late. The waves,
Building in the dark,
Slowly erase the beach.

You stand at the open
Window of the house,
Not knowing what to expect.

El elegido

Un año antes del día, designado era
El mancebo sin tacha, cuyo cuerpo,
Perfecto igual en proporción que en alma,
Mantenían en delicia, y aprendía
A tañer flautas, cortar cañas de humo,
Recoger flores, aspirando su aroma,
Con gracia cortesana a expresarse y moverse.

Estaba luego su jornada exenta
De otro cuidado, e iba, ocioso y libre,
Por la espalda la cabellera oscura,
Ornado de guirnaldas y metales
El cuerpo, como el de un dios ungido,
Y a su paso los otros en honor le tenían
Hasta besar la tierra que pisaba.

Veinte días antes del día, desnuda ahora
La piel de los perfumes, afeites y resinas,
El cabello cortado como aquel de un guerrero,
Las galas ya trocadas por más simple atavío,
Puro en el cuerpo como puro en la mente,
Cuatro doncellas bajo nombres de diosas
Para acceso carnal destinadas le eran.

Cinco días antes del día, las finales
Fiestas le aderezaban, en jardines
De la ciudad, el campo, la colina y el lago,
Por cuyas aguas iba la falúa entoldada,
Con él y sus mujeres, para darle consuelo
Antes de desertarle, y en la ribera opuesta
Quedaba solo al fin, sin afectos ni bienes.

The Chosen One

One year before the day, the unblemished
Youth was selected, his body
And soul perfectly in proportion,
Maintained in pleasure, and he learned
To play the flute, cut smoke-hued reeds,
And gather flowers, breathing in their scent,
And to express himself and move with courtly grace.

Then came his extended stay
In another city, and he went, free and at leisure,
His long dark hair flowing down his back,
His body adorned with garlands
And precious metals, like some anointed god,
And as he passed, others held him in honor,
Even kissing the ground on which he'd walked.

Now twenty days before the day, his skin
Stripped naked for the powders, resins and perfumes,
His hair cut like a warrior's,
Formal dress traded for simpler attire,
Pure in body as pure in mind,
Four virgins with the names of goddesses
Were destined to him for carnal consummation.

Five days before the day, the final
Festivals were mounted, in the city's
Gardens, in the countryside, the hills, the lake
On whose waters sailed the little covered boat
With him and his young women, to console him
Before deserting him, and on the far shore
He was alone at last, with neither loves nor goods.

Sobre cada escalón, en la pirámide del llano,
Cada una de las flautas tañidas por el gozo,
Rotas entre sus dedos, iban cayendo,
Hasta alcanzar el templo de la cima,
A cuyo umbral estaba el sacerdote:
Como una de sus cañas, allí, rota la vida,
Quedaba en su hermosura para siempre.

At each step of the pyramid on the plain,
Each of the flutes he'd played for pleasure
Fell, broken between his hands,
Until he reached the temple at the top,
Where at the threshold stood the priest:
There, like one of his reeds, his life cut short,
He in his beauty remained forever.

Amor en música

Aunque el tema sea el mismo,
Cada amor tiene su aire,
Que con tantas variaciones
Difiere y a nuevo sabe.

La primavera en los ojos
Lleva uno, y el verano
El otro en la piel, o al menos
Eso cree el enamorado.

Pero en todos el infierno
Está oculto, hasta el instante
De las lágrimas, del grito
Que de las entrañas sale.

Pues luego al infierno llevan,
Por eso a veces quisiste
Evitar sus paraísos
Con una prudencia triste.

Pero, amigo, ¿y a la música
Quién se niega, si es dotado
De oído bueno, ni al deseo
Ojos buenos que ven claro?

Si éstos nacen para locos
Y aquéllos para prudentes,
De qué lado estás ya sabes:
Canta tus aires fielmente.

Love in Music

Although the theme is constant,
Each love has its own tune,
Which varies from one to another
And has to be learned anew.

One of them carries spring
In his eyes, another summer
In his skin, or at least
That's what the smitten one thinks.

But in every one some hell
Is hidden, until it's time
For tears, for the cry
Coming out of your depths.

Knowing they drag you to hell,
Sometimes you tried to avoid
Their promised paradise
With a sad caution.

But friend, who can resist
Such music, if he's gifted
With a good ear, and who with clear
Eyes can deny desire?

If some were born for madness
And others for being cautious,
You know which side you're on:
You faithfully sing your songs.

Y deja la melodía
Llenarte todo el espíritu.
Ya qué más da gozo o pena
Si en el amor se han fundido.

And you allow the tune
To saturate your soul.
What else gives such joy or grief
As fused as they are in love.

País

Tus ojos son de donde
La nieve no ha manchado
La luz, y entre las palmas
El aire
Invisible es de claro.

Tu deseo es de donde
A los cuerpos se alía
Lo animal con la gracia
Secreta
De mirada y sonrisa.

Tu existir es de donde
Percibe el pensamiento,
Por la arena de mares
Amigos,
La eternidad en tiempo.

Country

Your eyes are from a place
Where snow has never stained
The light, and between the palms
The invisible
Air is clear.

Your desire is from a place
Where a secret animal
Grace is joined to
Bodies
In a smile or a glance.

Your being is from a place
Where thought perceives,
In friendly sands
And seas,
Eternity in time.

Versos para ti mismo

La noche y el camino. Mientras,
La cabeza recostada en tu hombro,
El cabello suave a flor de tu mejilla,
Su cuerpo duerme o sueña acaso.

No. Eres tú quien sueña solo
Aquel efecto noble compartido,
Cuyos ecos despiertan por tu mente desierta
Como en la concha los del mar que ya no existe.

Lines for Yourself

Night and the road. All the while
A head at rest on your shoulder,
Hair as soft as a flower at your cheek,
His body asleep or maybe dreaming.

No. It's you dreaming alone
Of that sublime shared feeling
Whose echoes are stirred in your deserted mind
The way a sea shell echoes an ocean that's gone.

Después

Y la primavera entonces
Ha de seguir, entreabriendo
En miradas fuego y sombra,
Espuma y aire en cabellos.

Otra vez el mismo encanto
De juventud por los miembros
Correrá, como una savia
De la hermosura en el tiempo.

Pero tú sombra sin cuerpo.

El amor de nuevo entonces
Ha de penetrar el pecho
De los amantes, con llaga
Suave, dulce cauterio.

Por él de pena y de gozo
Despertarán en su lecho
Otros ojos a la noche
Entre el placer y el tormento.

Mas tú sombra sin deseo.

Later

And spring will follow
Then, opening slowly
In glances of fire and shadow,
Hair full of sea-spray and sky.

Again the same spell
Of youth will course
Through your limbs, like beauty's
Sap pulsing in time.

But you are a bodyless shadow.

Then passion again will be
Piercing the breasts of
Lovers, leaving soft scars,
Sweet wounds cauterized.

For him full of sorrow and pleasure
Other eyes will be opening
Beside him in bed at night
In between pain and delight.

But you are a passionless shadow.

Lo más frágil es lo que dura

¿Tu mocedad? No es más
Que un olor de azahar

En plazuela a la tarde
Cuando la luz decae

Y algún farol se enciende.
Su perfume lo sientes

Alzarse de un pasado
Ayer tuyo, hoy extraño,

Envolviéndote: aroma
Único y sin memoria

De todo, sea la sangre,
Amores o amistades

En tu existir primero,
Cuando cualquier deseo

El tiempo pronto iba
A realizarlo un día

De aquel futuro; aroma
Furtivo como sombra,

Moviendo tus sentidos
Con un escalofrío.

The Most Fragile Thing Is What Endures

Your youth? It's no more
Than a scent of orange blossoms

In a little plaza some evening
When the light is fading

And a streetlamp is coming on.
You smell its perfume

Thrown up from a past
That was yours yesterday, remote today,

Enveloping you: a fragrance
Singular and immemorial

Of everything, your blood,
The loves and friendships

Of your first existence,
When whatever you desired

Would soon be made real
By time in that new

Future; a fragrance
Furtive as a shadow,

Stirring your senses
With a chill.

Y ves que es lo más hondo
De tu vivir un poco

De eso que llaman nada
Tantas gentes sensatas:

Un olor de azahar,
Aire. ¿Hubo algo más?

And you see the deepest thing
In your life is no more than a wisp

Of what so many sensible people
Would call nothing:

A scent of orange blossoms, air.
Was there ever anything more?

Poemas para un cuerpo

I
SALVADOR

Sálvale o condénale,
Porque ya su destino
Está en tus manos, abolido.

Si eres salvador, sálvale
De ti y de él; la violencia
De no ser uno en ti, aquiétala.

O si no lo eres, condénale,
Para que a su deseo
Suceda otro tormento.

Sálvale o condénale,
Pero así no le dejes
Seguir vivo, y perderte.

Poems for a Body

I
SAVIOR

Redeem him or condemn him,
Because now his fate
Is in your hands, abolished.

If you're a savior, save him
From you and from himself; relieve
The violence of not being one in you.

And if you're not, condemn him,
So his desire may
Succeed to some other torment.

Redeem him or condemn him,
But don't leave him like this
To go on living, and lose you.

II
Despedida

La calle, sola a medianoche,
Doblaba en eco vuestro paso.
Llegados a la esquina fue el momento;
Arma presta, el espacio.

Eras tú quien partía,
Fuiste primero tú el que rompiste,
Así el ánima rompe sola,
Con terror a ser libre.

Y entró la noche en ti, materia tuya
Su vastedad desierta,
Desnudo ya del cuerpo tan amigo
Que contigo uno era.

II
THE GOODBYE

The street, deserted at midnight,
Doubled your echoing footsteps.
At the corner it was time;
The drawn weapon, space.

You were the one who parted,
You were the first to break,
The way the spirit breaks out alone,
With all the terror of freedom.

And night came into you,
Its empty immensity yours,
Stripped now of the lover's body
That had been one with you.

III
PARA TI, PARA NADIE

Pues no basta el recuerdo,
Cuando aún queda tiempo,

Alguno que se aleja
Vuelve atrás la cabeza,

O aquel que ya se ha ido,
En algo posesivo,

Una carta, un retrato,
Los materiales rasgos

Busca, la fiel presencia
Con realidad terrena,

Y yo, este Luis Cernuda
Incógnito, que dura

Tan sólo un breve espacio
De amor esperanzado,

Antes que el plazo acabe
De vivir, a tu imagen

Tan querida me vuelvo
Aquí, en el pensamiento,

III
FOR YOU, FOR NO ONE

Memory isn't enough,
So, while there's still time,

Someone going away
Turns around to look,

Or the one already gone
Searches in something he has,

A letter, a picture,
Tangible traces,

Of the faithful presence
In earthly form,

And I, this unknown
Luis Cernuda, who lasts

For just a flash
Of hopeful love,

Before that opening
Closes, keep returning

In my thought to your
Image I adore,

Y aunque tú no has de verlas,
Para hablar con tu ausencia

Estas líneas escribo,
Únicamente por estar contigo.

And even though you won't read them,
I'm speaking with your absence,

Writing these lines solely
To be with you.

IV
SOMBRA DE MÍ

Bien sé yo que esta imagen
Fija siempre en la mente
No eres tú, sino sombra
Del amor que en mí existe
Antes que el tiempo acabe.

Mi amor así visible me pareces,
Por mí dotado de esa gracia misma
Que me hace sufrir, llorar, desesperarme
De todo a veces, mientras otras
Me levanta hasta el cielo en nuestra vida,
Sintiendo las dulzuras que se guardan
Sólo a los elegidos tras el mundo.

Y aunque conozco eso, luego pienso
Que sin ti, sin el raro
Pretexto que me diste,
Mi amor, que afuera está con su ternura,
Allá dentro de mí hoy seguiría
Dormido todavía y a la espera
De alguien que, a su llamada,
Le hiciera al fin latir gozosamente.

Entonces te doy gracias y te digo:
Para esto vine al mundo, y a esperarte;
Para vivir por ti, como tú vives
Por mí, aunque no lo sepas,
Por este amor tan hondo que te tengo.

IV
SHADOW OF MYSELF

I know very well this image
Fixed in my mind forever
Isn't you but a shadow
Of the love that's left in me
Before my time runs out.

That's how my love feels visible to me,
Invested by me with the very grace
That pains me, makes me despair and cry
Over everything sometimes, while at others
It lifts me to the sky right here in life,
Charged with those sweet feelings reserved
Only for the chosen across the world.

And while I know this I think
That if not for you, if not for the strange
Reason to live you gave me,
My love, out there with all its tenderness,
Would go on inside me now
Asleep and waiting
For someone whose call
Would make it come alive at last with pleasure.

That's why I thank you and say:
For this I came into the world, to wait for you,
To live for you, the way you live
For me, not even knowing it,
For the love I hold so deep in my soul for you.

V

EL AMANTE ESPERA

Y cuánto te importuno,
Señor, rogándote me vuelvas
Lo perdido, ya otras veces perdido
Y por ti recobrado para mí, que parece
Imposible guardarlo.

                    Nuevamente
Llamo a tu compasión, pues es la sola
Cosa que quiero bien, y tú la sola
Ayuda con que cuento.

                    Mas rogándote
Así, conozco que es pecado,
Ocasión de pecar lo que te pido,
Y aún no guardo silencio,
Ni me resigno al fin a la renuncia.

Tantos años vividos
En soledad y hastío, en hastío y pobreza,
Trajeron tras de ellos esta dicha,
Tan honda para mí, que así ya puedo
Justificar con ella lo pasado.

Por eso insisto aún, Señor, por eso vengo
De nuevo a ti, temiendo y aun seguro
De que si soy blasfemo me perdones:
Devuélveme, Señor, lo que he perdido,
El solo ser por quien vivir deseo.

V
THE LOVER WAITS

And how I beg you,
Lord, praying that you return to me
What's lost, already lost so often before
And restored by you for me, who seems
Incapable of keeping it.

Again
I appeal to your sympathy, as it's all
I really want, and you the only
Help I can count on.

I know it's a sin
To beg you like this,
But a chance to sin is what I'm asking for,
And I can't even keep it to myself,
Can't be resigned to giving it up for good.

So many years lived
Alone and disgusted, disgusted and poor,
Led to this happiness,
So deep that it even seems
To justify the past.

That's why I'm nagging, Lord, that's why I've come
To you one more time, afraid but certain
That if I'm taking your name in vain, you'll forgive me:
Lord, return to me what I've lost,
The only one for whom I want to live.

VI
Después de hablar

No sabes guardar silencio
Con tu amor. ¿Es que le importa
A los otros? Pues gozaste
Callado, callado ahora

Sufre, pero nada digas.
Es el amor de una esencia
Que se corrompe al hablarlo:
En el silencio se engendra,

Por el silencio se nutre
Y con silencio se abre
Como una flor. No lo digas;
Súfrelo en ti, pero cállate.

Si va a morir, con él muere;
Si va a vivir, con él vive.
Entre muerte y vida, calla,
Porque testigos no admite.

VI
After speaking

You don't know how to keep your love
To yourself. Does it matter
To anyone else? As you were happy
Quiet, now be quiet and

Suffer, and say nothing.
It's the kind of love
Corrupted when spoken of:
Engendered in silence,

Nurtured in silence
And in silence it opens
Like a flower. Don't say it;
Suffer it, but in silence.

If it's going to die, die with it;
If it's going to live, live with it.
Between living and dying, be quiet,
Because it admits no witness.

VII
HACIÉNDOSE TARDE

Entre los últimos brotes
La rosa no se ve rara,
Ni la alondra al levantarse
Atiende a que el sol retrasa,
O el racimo ya tardío
Cuida si es mustia la parra.
Pero tu cariño nuevo
La estación piensa acabada.

Pues la alondra con su canto
Siempre puebla la mañana
Y la rosa y el racimo
Siempre llenan la mirada,
Entonces, deja, no pienses
En que es tarde. ¿Hubo tardanza
Jamás para olor y zumo
O el revuelo de algún ala?

Fuerza las puertas del tiempo,
Amor que tan tarde llamas.

VII
LATE BLOOMING

In its final flowering
The rose doesn't feel strange,
Nor does the swallow soaring
To see the sun going down,
Nor do the last grapes
Care if the vine is withered.
And yet your new affection
Believes the season is over.

Just as the swallow keeps on
Filling the morning with song,
And the roses and the grapes
Go on filling your gaze,
Don't worry, don't believe
That it's too late. Was it ever
Too late for scent or juice
Or the flight of a wing?

The love that you summon late
Forces the gates of time.

VIII
VIVIENDO SUEÑOS

Tantos años que pasaron
Con mis soledades solo
Y hoy tú duermes a mi lado.

Son los caprichos del sino,
Aunque con sus circunloquios
Cuánto tiempo no he perdido.

Mas ahora en fin llegaste
De su mano, y aún no creo,
Despierto en el sueño, hallarte.

Oscura como la lluvia
Es tu existencia, y tus ojos,
Aunque dan luz, es oscura.

Pero de mí qué sería
Sin este pretexto tuyo
Que acompaña así la vida.

Miro y busco por la tierra:
Nada hay en ella que valga
Lo que tu sola presencia.

Cuando le parezca a alguno
Que entre lo mucho divago,
Poco de cariño supo.

VIII
Living one's dreams

So many years gone by
Alone with my solitudes
And now you're sleeping beside me.

Such are the whims of fate,
Even though with its twists
I didn't waste so much time.

But now at last you've come
From its hand, and I still can't believe,
Awake in this dream, I've found you.

Your being is dark
As the rain, and your eyes,
Though they sparkle, are dark.

But what would there be of me
Without this pretext of you
To keep my life company.

I look and I search the earth:
Nothing on it is worth
As much as your being here.

While it may seem to some
That I'm rambling aimlessly,
They know nothing of love.

Lo raro es que al mismo tiempo
Conozco que tú no existes
Fuera de mi pensamiento.

The strange thing is that I know
You have no other existence
Anywhere outside my thought.

IX
DE DÓNDE VIENES

Si alguna vez te oigo
Hablar de padre, madre, hermanos,
Mi imaginar no vence a la extrañeza
De que sea tu existir originado en otros,
En otros repetido,
Cuando único me parece,
Creado por mi amor; igual al árbol,
A la nube o al agua
Que están ahí, mas nuestros
Son y vienen de nosotros
Porque una vez les vimos
Como jamás les viera nadie antes.

Un puro conocer te dio la vida.

IX
Where you come from

If sometimes I hear you
Speak of your father, mother, brothers and sisters,
My imagination can't overcome the strangeness
Of your existence having begun in others,
Of there being others like you,
When you seem to me unique,
Created by my love; just like the tree,
The cloud or the water
Out there, but they're
Ours and they come from us
Because we saw them once
As no one saw them before.

A pure encounter brought you to life.

X
CONTIGO

¿Mi tierra?
Mi tierra eres tú.

¿Mi gente?
Mi gente eres tú.

El destierro y la muerte
Para mí están adonde
No estés tú.

¿Y mi vida?
Dime, mi vida,
¿Qué es, si no eres tú?

X
WITH YOU

My land?
My land is you.

My people?
You are my people.

Exile and death
For me are where
You are not.

And my life?
Tell me, my love,
What is it, if not you?

XI
El amante divaga

Acaso en el infierno el tiempo tenga
La ficción de medida que le damos
Aquí, o acaso tenga aquella desmesura
De momentos preciosos en la vida.
No sé. Mas allá el tiempo, según dicen,
Marcha hacia atrás, para irnos desviviendo.

Así esta historia nuestra, mía y tuya
(Mejor será decir nada más mía,
Aunque a tu parte queden la ocasión y el motivo,
Que no es poco), otra vez viviremos
Tú y yo (o viviré yo sólo),
De su fin al comienzo.

Extraño será entonces
Pasar de los principios del olvido
A aquel fervor iluso, cuando todo
Se animaba por ti, porque vivías,
Y de ahí a la ignorancia
De ti, anterior a nuestro hallazgo.

Pero en infiernos, de ese modo,
Dejaría de creer, y ni mismo tiempo
La idea de paraísos desechara;
Infierno y paraíso,
¿No serán cosa nuestra, de esta vida
Terrena a la que estamos hechos y es bastante?

XI
The lover digresses

Perhaps in hell time has
The fiction of measure we give it
Here, or maybe it has that timelessness
Of life's most precious moments.
Who knows. They say that in the beyond
Time flows backward, unliving us of our lives.

And so this story of ours, mine and yours
(Or more precisely nothing but mine,
Though you remain the occasion and the motive,
No small thing), we'll live it again,
You and I (or I'll live it alone),
From end to beginning.

It will be strange then
To go from the start of forgetting
To that illusory fervor when everything
Was brought to life by you, because you were alive,
And from there to not knowing
Of you, before we found each other.

But that way I'd cease to believe
In hell, and at the same time
Discard the idea of paradise;
Hell and paradise—
Aren't they in us, in this earthly life
We're made for, and isn't that enough?

Infierno y paraíso
Los creamos aquí, con nuestros actos
Donde el amor y el odio brotan juntos,
Animando el vivir. Y yo no quiero
Vida en la cual ya tú no tengas parte:
Olvido de ti, sí, mas no ignorancia tuya.

El camino que sube
Y el camino que baja
Uno y el mismo son; y mi deseo
Es que al fin de uno y de otro,
Con odio o con amor, con olvido o memoria,
Tu existir esté allí, mi infierno y paraíso.

We create hell
And paradise here, with what we do
Where love and hate spring up together
Bringing life alive. And I want
No life where there's no place for you:
I can forget you, yes, but not your unknowing me.

The way up
And the way down
Are one and the same; and my desire is,
For both of us, in the end,
Hating or loving, forgetting or remembering,
That you be there, my hell and paradise.

XII
La vida

Como cuando el sol enciende
Algún rincón de la tierra,
Su pobreza la redime,
Con risas verdes lo llena,

Así tu presencia viene
Sobre mi existencia oscura
A exaltarla, para darle
Esplendor, gozo, hermosura.

Pero también tú te pones
Lo mismo que el sol, y crecen
En torno mío las sombras
De soledad, vejez, muerte.

XII
LIFE

As when the sun lights up
Some corner of the land,
Redeeming its poverty,
Filling it with green laughter,

That's how your presence comes
Over my dark existence
To exalt it, to give it
Splendor, pleasure, beauty.

But you also go down
Just like the sun, and so
Grow the shadows around me
Of solitude, old age, death.

XIII
FIN DE LA APARIENCIA

Sin querer has deshecho
Cuanto mi vida era,
Menos el centro inmóvil
Del existir: la hondura
Fatal e insobornable.

Muchas veces temía
En mí y deseaba
El fin de esa apariencia
Que da valor al hombre
Para el hombre en el mundo.

Pero si deshiciste
Todo lo en mí prestado,
Me das así otra vida;
Y como ser primero
Inocente, estoy solo
Con mí mismo y contigo.

Aquel que da la vida,
La muerte da con ella.
Desasido del mundo
Por tu amor, me dejaste
Con mi vida y mi muerte.

XIII
End of appearances

Without even trying you've undone
Whatever my life was,
Except for the still center
Of being: the fatal
And inescapable depths.

Inwardly I often
Feared and desired
The end of appearances
That endow man with value
In the world of man.

But if you took from me
Everything I had,
You also renewed my life:
And just as I was innocent
At first, now I'm alone
With myself and with you.

Whoever gives life,
Gives death along with it.
Set free from the world
By your love, I'm left
With my life and my death.

Morir parece fácil,
La vida es lo difícil:
Ya no sé sino usarla
En ti, con este inútil
Trabajo de quererte,
Que tú no necesitas.

Dying seems easy enough,
It's living that's hard:
I don't know what use it is
Except with you, with this useless
Labor of loving you,
Which you've no use for.

XIV
Precio de un cuerpo

Cuando algún cuerpo hermoso,
Como el tuyo, nos lleva
Tras de sí, él mismo no comprende,
Sólo el amante y el amor lo saben.
(Amor, terror de soledad humana.)

Esta humillante servidumbre,
Necesidad de gastar la ternura
En un ser que llenamos
Con nuestro pensamiento,
Vivo de nuestra vida.

Él da el motivo,
Lo diste tú; porque tú existes
Afuera como sombra de algo,
Una sombra perfecta
De aquel afán, que es del amante, mío.

Si yo te hablase
Cómo el amor depara
Su razón al vivir y su locura,
Tú no comprenderías.
Por eso nada digo.

La hermosura, inconsciente
De su propia celada, cobró la presa
Y sigue. Así, por cada instante
De goce, el precio está pagado:
Este infierno de angustia y de deseo.

XIV
COST OF A BODY

When a beautiful body
Like yours pulls us
Into its orbit, it doesn't have any idea,
Only the lover and love are aware.
(Love, terror of human solitude.)

This humiliating servitude,
The need to be tender
To someone we fill
With our thought,
Alive with our life.

It provides its own motive,
You said so yourself; because you exist
Out there like the shadow of something,
A perfect shadow
Of that hot want, the lover's, mine.

If I spoke to you
The way love provides
Its reason for living and its madness,
You wouldn't understand.
And so I say nothing.

Beauty, unconscious
That it's a trap, collects its prey
And keeps on. And so, for every moment
Of pleasure, the price is paid:
This hell of anguish and longing.

XV
Divinidad celosa

Los cuatro elementos primarios
Dan forma a mi existir:
Un cuerpo sometido al tiempo,
Siempre ansioso de ti.

Porque el tiempo de amor nos vale
Toda una eternidad
Donde ya el hombre no va solo,
Y Dios celoso está.

Déjame amarte ahora. Un día,
Temprano o tarde, Dios
Dispone que el amante deba
Renunciar a su amor.

XV
A jealous God

The four prime elements
Give form to my existence:
A body subject to time,
Ever eager for you.

Because the time of love is worth
A whole eternity
Where for once we're not alone,
And God himself is jealous.

Let me love you now. One day,
Sooner or later, God
Will force the lover
To renounce his love.

XVI
Un hombre con su amor

Si todo fuera dicho
Y entre tú y yo la cuenta
Se saldara, aún tendría
Con tu cuerpo una deuda.

Pues ¿quién pondría precio
A esta paz, olvidado
En ti, que al fin conocen
Mis labios por tus labios?

En tregua con la vida,
No saber, querer nada,
Ni esperar: tu presencia
Y mi amor. Eso basta.

Tú y mi amor, mientras miro
Dormir tu cuerpo cuando
Amanece. Así mira
Un dios lo que ha creado.

Mas mi amor nada puede
Sin que tu cuerpo acceda:
Él sólo informa un mito
En tu hermosa materia.

XVI
A MAN WITH HIS LOVE

If all were said and done
And between the two of us accounts
Were settled, I'd still owe
A debt to your body.

Then who could put a price
On this peace, forgotten
By you, that my lips have known
Through yours.

In a truce with life,
Knowing and wanting nothing,
Expecting nothing: your presence
And my love. This is enough.

You and my love, while I watch
Your body sleeping, the sun
Rising. That's how a god
Must look on his creation.

But my love can do nothing
Unless your body agrees:
It alone, your physical beauty,
Puts flesh on a myth.

From

Desolación de la Quimera

Desolation of the Chimera

[1956–1962]

Las sirenas

Ninguno ha conocido la lengua en la que cantan las sirenas
Y pocos los que acaso, al oír algún canto a medianoche
(No en el mar, tierra adentro, entre las aguas
De un lago), creyeron ver a una friolenta
Y triste surgir como fantasma y entonarles
Aquella canción misma que resistiera Ulises.

Cuando la noche acaba y tiempo ya no hay
A cuanto se esperó en las horas de un día,
Vuelven los que las vieron: mas la canción quedaba,
Filtro, poción de lágrimas, embebida en su espíritu,
Y sentían en sí con resonancia honda
El encanto en el canto de la sirena envejecida.

Escuchado tan bien y con pasión tanta oído,
Ya no eran los mismos y otro vivir buscaron,
Posesos por el filtro que enfebreció su sangre.
¿Una sola canción puede cambiar así una vida?
El canto había cesado, las sirenas callado, y sus ecos.
El que una vez las oye viudo y desolado queda para siempre.

The Sirens

No one has ever understood the language the sirens sing
And few are those who by chance, on hearing some song at midnight
(Not out at sea, but inland, from the waters
Of a lake), believed they saw a shivering
And mournful ghostlike thing appear and sing them
That same song Ulysses might have resisted.

When the night ends and there's no more time
For all that was hoped for in a day's hours,
The ones who saw them returned: but the song remained,
A potion, a brew of tears, imbibed in their spirit,
And they felt resounding deep inside themselves
The spell in the song of the tired old siren.

Having heard so much so well and with such passion,
They were no longer the same and they sought another life,
Possessed by the potion that set their blood ablaze.
Can a single song so change the way one lives?
The singing had ceased, the sirens quieted, and their echoes.
But he who hears them once remains forever desolate and widowed.

Niño tras un cristal

Al caer la tarde, absorto
Tras el cristal, el niño mira
Llover. La luz que se ha encendido
En un farol contrasta
La lluvia blanca con el aire oscuro.

La habitación a solas
Le envuelve tibiamente,
Y el visillo, velando
Sobre el cristal, como una nube,
Le susurra lunar encantamiento.

El colegio se aleja. Es ahora
La tregua, con el libro
De historias y de estampas
Bajo la lámpara, la noche,
El sueño, las horas sin medida.

Vive en el seno de su fuerza tierna,
Todavía sin deseo, sin memoria,
El niño, y sin presagio
Que afuera el tiempo aguarda
Con la vida, al acecho.

En su sombra ya se forma la perla.

Child Behind a Window

At nightfall, lost in thought
Behind the window, the little boy watches
The rain. The light coming on
In a streetlamp contrasts
The white rain against the darkening air.

The solitary room
Surrounds him warmly,
And the sheer curtain, veiling
The glass, like a cloud,
Whispers a lunar spell.

School drifts away. Now it's time
For a break, with the book
Of stories and pictures
Under the lamp, night,
Dreams, the unmeasured hours.

He lives in the heart of his tender strength,
As yet without desire, without memory,
The child, not yet knowing
That outside time is waiting
With life, in ambush.

In his shadow the pearl is already forming.

Mozart

[1756-1956]

I

Si alguno alguna vez te preguntase:
"La música, ¿qué es?" "Mozart", dirías,
"Es la música misma." Sí, el cuerpo entero
De la armonía impalpable e invisible,
Pero del cual oímos su paso susurrante
De linfa, con el frescor que dan lunas y auroras,
En cascadas creciendo, en ríos caudalosos.

Desde la tierra mítica de Grecia
Llegó hasta el norte el soplo que la anima
Y en el norte halló eco, entre las voces
De poetas, filósofos y músicos: ciencia
Del ver, ciencia del saber, ciencia del oír. Mozart
Es la gloria de Europa, el ejemplo más alto
De la gloria del mundo, porque Europa es el mundo.

Cuando vivió, entreoído en las cortes,
Los palacios, donde príncipes y prelados
Poder, riqueza detentaban nulos,
Mozart entretenía, como siempre ocurre,
Como es fatal que ocurra al genio, aunque ya toque
A su cénit. Cuando murió, supieron todos:
Cómo admiran las gentes al genio una vez muerto.

Mozart
[1756-1956]

I

If sometime someone were to ask you:
"What is music?" "Mozart," you'd say,
"Is music itself." Yes, the whole body
Of impalpable invisible harmony,
The limpid sound of whose stream
We hear, with the coolness of moons and dawns,
In gushing waterfalls, in rushing rivers.

From the mythic land of Greece
A breeze came north and found
An echo, came alive in northern voices
Of poets, thinkers, musicians: a science
Of seeing, science of knowing, science of hearing. Mozart
Is Europe's glory, the peak
Of the world's glory, as Europe is the world.

When he was alive, misheard in the courts,
The palaces, where princes and prelates,
Power and riches uselessly ruled,
Mozart entertained, as always happens,
As fatally happens to genius, no matter
How great. When he died, they all understood:
The way people always admire a dead genius.

II

De su tiempo es su genio, y del nuestro, y de siempre.
Nítido el tema, preciso el desarrollo,
Un ala y otra ala son, que reposadas
Por el círculo oscuro de los instrumentistas,
Arpa, violín, flauta, piano, luego a otro
Firmamento más glorioso y más fresco
Desplegasen súbitamente en música.

Toda razón su obra, pero sirviendo toda
Imaginación, en sí gracia y majestad une,
Ironía y pasión, hondura y ligereza.
Su arquitectura deshelada, formas líquidas
Da de esplendor inexplicable, y así traza
Vergeles encantados, mágicos alcázares,
Fluidos bajo un frío rielar de estrellas.

Su canto, la mocedad toda en él lo canta:
Ya mano que acaricia o ya garra que hiere,
Arrullo tierno en sarcasmo de sí mismo,
Es (como ante el ceño de la muerte
Los juegos del amor, el dulce monstruo rubio)
Burla de la pasión que nunca halla respuesta,
Sabiendo su poder y su fracaso eterno.

II

His genius is of his time, and ours, and always.
The bright theme, the precise unfolding,
A pair of wings at rest
In the dark circle of players,
Harp, violin, flute, piano, then suddenly
Musically taking flight into a fresher
More glorious sky.

His work is all reason, yet in the service of all
Imagination, a fusion of grace and majesty,
Passion and irony, depth and lightness.
Its melted architecture pours forth liquid forms
Of inexplicable splendor, tracing
Enchanted gardens, magical castles,
Fluid beneath an icy shimmer of stars.

His song is replete with the power of youth:
Now a caressing hand and now a tearing claw,
A tender cooing that mocks itself;
It is (like the play of love, that sweet
Blond monster, facing the gloom of death)
A passionate joke that has no answer,
Knowing its force and its eternal failure.

III

En cualquier urbe oscura, donde amortaja el humo
Al sueño de un vivir urdido en la costumbre
Y el trabajo no da libertad ni esperanza,
Aún queda la sala del concierto, aún puede el hombre
Dejar que su mente humillada se ennoblezca
Con la armonía sin par, el arte inmaculado
De esta voz de la música que es Mozart.

Si de manos de Dios informe salió el mundo,
Trastornado su orden, su injusticia terrible;
Si la vida es abyecta y ruin el hombre,
Da esta música al mundo forma, orden, justicia,
Nobleza y hermosura. Su salvador entonces
¿Quién es? Su redentor ¿quién es entonces?
Ningún pecado en él, ni martirio, ni sangre.

Voz más divina que otra alguna, humana
Al mismo tiempo, podemos siempre oírla,
Dejarla que despierte sueños idos
Del ser que fuimos y al vivir matamos.
Sí, el hombre pasa, pero su voz perdura,
Nocturno ruiseñor o alondra mañanera,
Sonando en las ruinas del cielo de los dioses.

III

In any murky city, where smoke
Shrouds the dreams of a life warped by convention
And work gives neither freedom nor any hope,
There's still the concert hall, a man can still
Let his humiliated mind be dignified
By peerless harmony, the immaculate art
Of this voice of music that is Mozart.

If the world was delivered formless from God's hands,
Its order twisted, its injustice hideous;
If life is pitiful and man contemptible,
This music gives the world form, order, justice,
Dignity and beauty. Its savior then,
Who is it? Its redeemer, who is it then?
No sin in him, no martyrdom, no gore.

Voice more divine than any other, human
All the same, we can always hear it,
Let it awaken our lost dreams
Of the being we were and killed in the course of living.
Yes, man disappears, but his voice endures,
An evening nightingale or morning swallow
Sounding in the ruins of the gods' heaven.

Bagatela

Como un pájaro de fuego
La luna está entre las ramas
Del enebro.

Negro es el cuerpo del árbol
Y gris el aire nocturno,
Oro el astro.

Dios por lo visto hace muestra
Que ha oído de alguna estampa
Japonesa.

Bagatelle

Like a firebird
The moon perches in the branches
Of the juniper.

The tree trunk is black,
The night air gray,
The moon gold.

This is God's way of showing
That he's heard tell of some
Japanese print.

A propósito de flores

Era un poeta joven, apenas conocido.
En su salida primera al mundo
Buscaba alivio a su dolencia
Cuando muere en Roma, entre sus manos una carta,
La última carta, que ni abrir siquiera quiso,
De su amor jamás gozado.

El amigo que en la muerte le asistiera
Sus palabras finales nos trasmite:
"Ver cómo crece alguna flor menuda,
El crecer silencioso de las flores,
Acaso fue la única dicha
Que he tenido en el mundo."

¿Pureza? Vivo, a las flores amadas contemplaba
Y mucho habló de ellas en sus versos;
En el trance final su mente se volvía
A la dicha más pura que conoció en la vida:
Ver a la flor que abre, su color y su gracia.

¿Amargura? Vivo, sinsabores tuvo
Amargos que apurar, sus breves años
Apenas conocieron momentos sin la sombra.
En la muerte quiso volverse con tácito sarcasmo
A la felicidad de la flor que entreabre.

¿Amargura? ¿Pureza? ¿O, por qué no, ambas a un tiempo?
El lirio se corrompe como la hierba mala
Y el poeta no es puro o amargo únicamente:
Devuelve sólo al mundo lo que el mundo le ha dado,
Aunque su genio amargo y puro algo más le regale.

With Regard to Flowers

He was a young poet, barely known.
On his first venture into the world
In search of relief from his illness
He dies in Rome, a letter in his hand,
The last, unopened letter from his love
With whom he'd never had the pleasure.

The friend who was with him at his death
Passes along to us his final words:
To watch the way some little flower grows,
The quiet growing of the flowers,
May well have been the only happiness
I've ever had in the world.

Purity of heart? Alive, he regarded his beloved flowers
And often wrote about them in his verses;
In his final delirium his mind returned
To the purest happiness he'd known in life:
To watch a flower opening, its color and its grace.

Bitterness? Alive, he had his heartaches
Bitter to swallow, his brief years
Barely knew a few minutes out of the shadows.
Dying, he tried to return with tacit sarcasm
To the happiness of the slowly opening flower.

Bitterness? Purity of heart? Or why not both at once?
The lily withers the same as the weeds,
And the poet is neither wholly pure nor bitter:
He gives back to the world only what the world has given him,
Though his pure and bitter genius may give something more.

Birds in the night

El gobierno francés, ¿o fue el gobierno inglés?, puso una lápida
En esa casa 8 Great College Street, Camden Town, Londres,
Adonde en una habitación Rimbaud y Verlaine, rara pareja,
Vivieron, bebieron, trabajaron, fornicaron,
Durante algunas breves semanas tormentosas.
Al acto inaugural asistieron sin duda embajador y alcalde,
Todos aquellos que fueran enemigos de Verlaine y Rimbaud cuando vivían.

La casa es triste y pobre, como el barrio,
Con la tristeza sórdida que va con lo que es pobre,
No la tristeza funeral de lo que es rico sin espíritu.
Cuando la tarde cae, como en el tiempo de ellos,
Sobre su acera, húmedo y gris el aire, un organillo
Suena, y los vecinos, de vuelta del trabajo,
Bailan unos, los jóvenes, los otros van a la taberna.

Corta fue la amistad singular de Verlaine el borracho
Y de Rimbaud el golfo, querellándose largamente.
Mas podemos pensar que acaso un buen instante
Hubo para los dos, al menos si recordaba cada uno
Que dejaron atrás la madre inaguantable y la aburrida esposa.
Pero la libertad no es de este mundo, y los libertos,
En ruptura con todo, tuvieron que pagarla a precio alto.

Sí, estuvieron ahí, la lápida lo dice, tras el muro,
Presos de su destino: la amistad imposible, la amargura
De la separación, el escándalo luego; y para éste
El proceso, la cárcel por dos años, gracias a sus costumbres
Que sociedad y ley condenan, hoy al menos; para aquél a solas
Errar desde un rincón a otro de la tierra,
Huyendo a nuestro mundo y su progreso renombrado.

Birds in the Night

The French—or was it the English?—government placed a plaque
On that house at 8 Great College Street, Camden Town, London,
Where in a room Rimbaud and Verlaine, a peculiar couple,
Lived, drank, worked, and fornicated
For a few brief stormy weeks.
No doubt the ambassador and the mayor attended the dedication,
All the same people who were enemies of Rimbaud and Verlaine when they lived.

The house is sad and poor, like the neighborhood,
With the sordid sadness that goes with poverty,
Not the funereal sadness of spiritless wealth.
When night comes down, as in their time,
Over that sidewalk, with its damp gray air, a hand organ
Plays, and the neighbors, on their way home from work,
The young ones dance, the rest take to the pub.

Brief was the singular friendship of Verlaine the drunk
And Rimbaud the tramp, quarreling constantly.
But we can think that maybe it was
A good time for the two, at least if each remembered
That they left behind an intolerable mother and a boring wife.
But freedom is not of this world, and the freed,
Having broken with everything, had a high price to pay.

Yes, they were there, the plaque says so, behind the wall,
Prisoners of their fate: the impossible friendship, the bitterness
Of separation, and then the scandal; and for this one
The trial, and two years in jail, thanks to his habits
Condemned by society and law, at least up to now; for that one on his own
To wander from one corner of the earth to the other,
Escaping to our world and its celebrated progress.

El silencio del uno y la locuacidad banal del otro
Se compensaron. Rimbaud rechazó la mano que oprimía
Su vida; Verlaine la besa, aceptando su castigo.
Uno arrastra en el cinto el oro que ha ganado; el otro
Lo malgasta en ajenjo y mujerzuelas. Pero ambos
En entredicho siempre de las autoridades, de la gente
Que con trabajo ajeno se enriquece y triunfa.

Entonces hasta la negra prostituta tenía derecho de insultarles;
Hoy, como el tiempo ha pasado, como pasa en el mundo,
Vida al margen de todo, sodomía, borrachera, versos escarnecidos,
Ya no importan en ellos, y Francia usa de ambos nombres y ambas obras
Para mayor gloria de Francia y su arte lógico.
Sus actos y sus pasos se investigan, dando al público
Detalles íntimos de sus vidas. Nadie se asusta ahora, ni protesta.

"¿Verlaine? Vaya, amigo mío, un sátiro, un verdadero sátiro
Cuando de la mujer se trata; bien normal era el hombre,
Igual que usted y que yo. ¿Rimbaud? Católico sincero, como está demostrado."
Y se recitan trozos del "Barco ebrio" y del soneto a las "Vocales".
Mas de Verlaine no se recita nada, porque no está de moda
Como el otro, del que se lanzan textos falsos en edición de lujo;
Poetas jóvenes, por todos los países, hablan mucho de él en sus provincias.

¿Oyen los muertos lo que los vivos dicen luego de ellos?
Ojalá nada oigan: ha de ser un alivio ese silencio interminable
Para aquellos que vivieron por la palabra y murieron por ella,
Como Rimbaud y Verlaine. Pero el silencio allá no evita
Acá la farsa elogiosa repugnante. Alguna vez deseó uno
Que la humanidad tuviese una sola cabeza, para así cortársela.
Tal vez exageraba: si fuera sólo una cucaracha, y aplastarla.

The silence of one and the talkative banality of the other
Made for a kind of balance. Rimbaud rejected the hand that oppressed
His life; Verlaine kisses it, accepting his punishment.
One drags in his belt the gold he's gained; the other
Wastes it on absinthe and whores. But both
Outside the law forever, beyond the respectable people
Whose meaningless work makes them rich and successful.

Then even the black prostitute had the right to insult them;
Today, as time has passed, as it does in the world,
Their lives on the edge of everything, sodomy, drunkenness, vicious verses,
No longer matter, and France makes use of both their names and their works
For the greater glory of France and its logical art.
Their acts and their comings and goings are studied, giving the public
Intimate tidbits about their lives. No one is shocked now, nor protests.

"Verlaine? Go on, my friend, a satyr, a regular lech
When it comes to women; a perfectly normal fellow,
Like you and I. Rimbaud? A devout Catholic, as it's been proved."
And they recite hunks of the "Drunken Boat" and the sonnet to the "Vowels."
But of Verlaine they recite nothing, because he's not in vogue
Like the other, of whom they bring out phony texts in fancy editions;
Young poets, in every country, talk about him nonstop in their provinces.

Can the dead hear what the living are saying about them?
Let's hope not: that endless silence must be a relief
For those who lived and died by the word,
Like Rimbaud and Verlaine. But the silence there is no escape
From this repugnant laudatory farce. There was a time one of them wished
That humanity had a single head, so it could be chopped off.
Maybe he was exaggerating: if it were just a cockroach, and be crushed.

Otra vez, con sentimiento

Ya no creí que más invocaría
De tu amistad antigua la memoria,
Que de ti se adueñó toda una tribu
Extraña para mí y para ti no menos
Extraña acaso.

       Mas uno de esa tribu,
Profesor y, según pretenden él y otros
De por allá (cuánto ha caído nuestra tierra),
Poeta, te ha llamado "mi príncipe".
Y me pregunto qué hiciste tú para que ése
Pueda considerarte como príncipe suyo.

¿Vaciedad académica? La vaciedad común resulta
En sus escritos. Mas su rapto retórico
No aclara a nuestro entendimiento
Lo secreto en tu obra, aunque también le llamen
Crítico de la poesía nuestra contemporánea.

La apropiación de ti, que nada suyo
Fuiste o quisiste ser mientras vivías,
Es lo que ahí despierta mi extrañeza.
¿Príncipe tú de un sapo? ¿No les basta
A tus compatriotas haberte asesinado?

Ahora la estupidez sucede al crimen.

Once More, with Feeling

From our old friendship
I never thought I'd ever remember again
How a whole tribe, such a strange group
To me and maybe no less strange to you,
Adopted you.

           But one of that tribe,
A professor and, according to him and others
Over there (which shows how far our land has fallen),
A poet, called you "my prince."
And I ask myself what you ever did that he
Could have come to think of you as his prince.

Academic claptrap? His writings are full of clichés
And conventional thinking. But his rapturous rhetoric
Does nothing to clarify our understanding
Of the mystery in your work, even though he's also called
A critic of our contemporary poetry.

The appropriation of you, which you wanted
Nothing to do with when you were alive,
Is what now seems to me so utterly strange.
The prince of a toad? Isn't it enough
For your countrymen to have killed you?

And now stupidity succeeds the crime.

Música cautiva

A dos voces

"Tus ojos son los ojos de un hombre enamorado;
Tus labios son los labios de un hombre que no cree
En el amor." "Entonces, dime el remedio, amigo,
Si están en desacuerdo realidad y deseo."

Captive Music

for two voices

"Your eyes are the eyes of a man in love; but
Your lips are the lips of a man who doesn't believe
In love." "So what can you do, my friend,
If reality and desire are at odds."

Antes de irse

Más no pedí de ti,
Tú mundo sin virtud,
Que en el aire y en mí
Un pedazo de azul.

A otros la ambición
De fortuna y poder;
Yo sólo quise ser
Con mi luz y mi amor.

Before Going Away

I asked no more of you,
Your world virtue free,
Than in the air and in me
A little bit of blue.

Let others crave the might
Of money and success;
I wanted just to be
With my love and my light.

Pregunta vieja, vieja respuesta

¿Adonde va el amor cuando se olvida?
No aquel a quien hicieras la pregunta
Es quien hoy te responde.

Es otro, al que unos años más de vida
Le dieron la ocasión, que no tuviste,
De hallar una respuesta.

Los juguetes del niño que ya es hombre,
¿Adonde fueron, di? Tú lo sabías,
Bien pudiste saberlo.

Nada queda de ellos: sus ruinas
Informes e incoloras, entre el polvo,
El tiempo se ha llevado.

El hombre que envejece, halla en su mente,
En su deseo, vacíos, sin encanto,
Dónde van los amores.

Mas si muere el amor, no queda libre
El hombre del amor: queda su sombra,
Queda en pie la lujuria.

¿Adonde va el amor cuando se olvida?
No aquel a quien hicieras la pregunta
Es quien hoy te responde.

Old Question, Old Answer

Where does love go once it's forgotten?
The person to whom you posed the question
Isn't the one who's answering you now.

He's someone else, who's lived a few more years
And so been given the chance, which he didn't have
Before, to find the answer.

The toys of a child who has now grown up,
Tell me, where did they disappear? You knew,
You knew so well.

Nothing's left of them: their broken pieces
Crumbling and faded, gathering dust,
Were blown away by time.

A man as he grows old finds in his mind,
In his desire, empty pleasureless spaces
Where his loves have gone.

But even when love has died, the man
Is never free of love: its shadow lingers,
Desire endures.

Where does love go once it's forgotten?
The person to whom you posed the question
Is not the one who's answering you now.

Luis de Baviera escucha Lohengrin

Sólo dos tonos rompen la penumbra:
Destellar de algún oro y estridencia granate.
Al fondo luce la caverna mágica
Donde unas criaturas, ¿de qué naturaleza?, pasan
Melodiosas, manando de sus voces música
Que, con fuente escondida, lenta fluye
O, crespa luego, su caudal agita
Estremeciendo el aire fulvo de la cueva
Y con iris perlado riela en notas.

Sombras la sala de auditorio nulo.
En el palco real un elfo solo asiste
Al festejo del cual razón parece dar y enigma:
Negro pelo, ojos sombríos que contemplan
La gruta luminosa, en pasmo friolento
Esculpido. La pelliza de martas le agasaja
Abierta a una blancura, a seda que se anuda en lazo.
Los ojos entornados escuchan, beben la melodía
Como una tierra seca absorbe el don del agua.

Asiste a doble fiesta: una exterior, aquella
De que es testigo, otra interior allá en su mente,
Donde ambas se funden (como color y forma
Se funden en un cuerpo), componen una misma delicia.
Así, razón y enigma, el poder le permite
A solas escuchar las voces a su orden concertadas,
El brotar melodioso que le acuna y nutre
Los sueños, mientras la escena desarrolla,
Ascua litúrgica, una amada leyenda.

Louis of Bavaria Listens to Lohengrin

Just two tones break through the darkness:
A golden explosion and a blood-red shriek.
In the background glows the magic cavern
Where some creatures—what kind?—move
Melodiously, their voices dripping with music
Which, from a hidden source, flows slowly
Then curling, changes its level,
Shaking the murky air of the cave,
And shimmers in notes of pearly iridescence.

The shadowy auditorium is empty.
In the royal box a lone elf attends
The festivities of which he is occasion and enigma:
Black hair, dark eyes that contemplate
The shining grotto sculpted in shivering
Shockwaves. The sable coat bestowed on him in his honor
Opens to show a whiteness, a silk bow tie.
His eyes turned inward listen, drink in the melody
As a land in drought absorbs the gift of water.

He's attending a double performance: one out there, the one
He's witnessing, the other inward, there in his mind,
And where both converge (as color and form
Converge in a body), they make for a single pleasure.
And so, occasion and enigma, power allows him
To listen alone to the voices assembled on his order,
The melodious flow that rocks him and feeds
His dreams, while the scene unrolls,
A liturgical ember, a beloved legend.

Ni existe el mundo, ni la presencia humana
Interrumpe el encanto de reinar en sueños.
Pero, mañana, chambelán, consejero, ministro,
Volverán con demandas estúpidas al rey:
Que gobierne por fin, les oiga y les atienda.
¿Gobernar? ¿Quién gobierna en el mundo de los sueños?
¿Cuándo llegará el día en que gobiernen los lacayos?
Se interpondrá un biombo, benéfico, entre el rey y sus ministros.
Un elfo corre libre los bosques, bebe el aire.

Ésa es la vida, y trata fielmente de vivirla:
Que le dejen vivirla. No en la ciudad, el nido
Ya está sobre las cimas nevadas de las sierras
Más altas de su reino. Carretela, trineo,
Por las sendas; flotilla nivea, por los ríos y lagos,
Le esperan siempre, prestos a levantarle
Adonde vive su reino verdadero, que no es de este mundo:
Donde el sueño le espera, donde la soledad le aguarda,
Donde la soledad y el sueño le ciñen su única corona.

Mas la presencia humana es a veces encanto,
Encanto imperioso que el rey mismo conoce
Y sufre con tormento inefable: el bisel de una boca,
Unos ojos profundos, una piel soleada,
Gracia de un cuerpo joven. Él lo conoce,
Sí, lo ha conocido, y cuántas veces padecido,
El imperio que ejerce la criatura joven,
Obrando sobre él, dejándole indefenso,
Ya no rey, sino siervo de la humana hermosura.

The world has ceased to exist, not a human presence
Interrupts the spell of reigning in dreams.
But tomorrow chamberlain, counselor, minister
Will return to the king with their stupid demands:
He has to govern, and so must listen, pay attention.
Govern? Who can govern in the world of dreams?
When will the day come when the lackeys govern?
There'll be a beneficent screen between the king and his ministers.
An elf runs free through the woods and gulps the air.

That's life, and he tries faithfully to live it:
May they let him live it. Not in the city, his nest
Is already on the snowy peaks of the tallest
Mountains in his kingdom. A cart, a sledge
On the trails; a snowy flotilla on the rivers and lakes,
Always awaiting him, ready to take him
Where his real kingdom resides, which is not of this world:
Where dreams await him, where solitude protects him,
Where solitude and dreams enwrap him in his only crown.

But human presence too can cast a spell,
An imperious spell known to the king himself
And which he has ineffably suffered: the bevel of a mouth,
Deep eyes, sun-browned skin,
The grace of a young body. He knows it,
Yes, he's known it, and how often suffered
The rule exerted by a youthful creature
Working him over, leaving him defenseless,
No longer king but slave to human beauty.

Flotando sobre música el sueño ahora se encarna:
Mancebo todo blanco, rubio, hermoso, que llega
Hacia él y que es él mismo. ¿Magia o espejismo?
¿Es posible a la música dar forma, ser forma de mortal alguno?
¿Cuál de los dos es él, o no es él, acaso, ambos?
El rey no puede, ni aun pudiendo quiere dividirse a sí del otro
Sobre la música inclinado, como extraño contempla
Con emoción gemela su imagen desdoblada
Y en éxtasis de amor y melodía queda suspenso.

Él es el otro, desconocido hermano cuyo existir jamás creyera
Ver algún día. Ahora ahí está y en él ya ama
Aquello que en él mismo pretendieron amar otros.
Con su canto le llama y le seduce. Pero, ¿puede
Consigo mismo unirse? Teme que, si respira, el sueño escape.
Luego un terror le invade: ¿no muere aquel que ve a su doble?
La fuerza del amor, bien despierto ya en él, alza su escudo
Contra todo temor, debilidad, desconfianza.
Como Elsa, ama, mas sin saber a quién. Sólo sabe que ama.

En el canto, palabra y movimiento de los labios
Del otro le habla también el canto, palabra y movimiento
Que a brotar de sus labios al mismo tiempo iban,
Saludando al hermano nacido de su sueño, nutrido por su sueño.
Mas no, no es eso: es la música quien nutriera a su sueño, le dio forma.
Su sangre se apresura en sus venas, al tiempo apresurando:
El pasado, tan breve, revive en el presente,
Con luz de dioses su presente ilumina al futuro.
Todo, todo ha de ser como su sueño le presagia.

Floating on the music the dream takes flesh:
A white-skinned youth, blond, beautiful, who comes
Toward him and is he himself. Magic or mirage?
Is it possible to give form to music, for it to be a form of someone mortal?
Which of the two is he, or is he not, possibly, both?
The king cannot, nor if he could would want to divide himself from the other,
Leaning into the music, as someone else regards
With twinned emotion his doubled image
In loving ecstasy and melody held suspended.

He is the other, unknown brother whose existence he never thought
He'd see. Now there he is and in him he loves
That in himself which others pretended to love.
With his song he summons and seduces him. But can
He come together with himself? He fears that, if he breathes, the dream
    may escape.
Then he's filled with terror: does not whoever sees his double, die?
The power of love, now fully awake in him, throws up its shield
Against all fear, all weakness, lack of confidence.
Like Elsa, he loves, but without knowing whom. He only knows he loves.

In the song, the words, the movement of the lips
Of the other the song, the words, the movement
That sprang from his lips at the same time,
Greeting the brother born from his dream, fed by his dream,
But no, it's not that: it's the music that nurtured his dream, that gave it form.
His blood races faster in his veins, speeding up time:
The past, so brief, comes back alive in the present,
With godlike light his present illumines the future.
Everything, everything is to be as his dream presages.

En el vivir del otro el suyo certidumbre encuentra.
Sólo el amor depara al rey razón para estar vivo,
Olvido a su impotencia, saciedad al deseo
Vago y disperso que tanto tiempo le aquejara.
Se inclina y se contempla en la corriente
Melodiosa e, imagen ajenada, su remedio espera
Al trastorno profundo que dentro de sí siente.
¿No le basta que exista, fuera de él, lo amado?
Contemplar a lo hermoso, ¿no es respuesta bastante?

Los dioses escucharon, y su deseo satisfacen
(Que los dioses castigan concediendo a los hombres
Lo que éstos les piden), y el destino del rey,
Desearse a sí mismo, le trasforma,
Como en flor, en cosa hermosa, inerme, inoperante,
Hasta acabar su vida gobernado por lacayos,
Pero teniendo en ellos, al morir, la venganza de un rey.
Las sombras de sus sueños para él eran la verdad de la vida.
No fue de nadie, ni a nadie pudo llamar suyo.

Ahora el rey está ahí, en su palco, y solitario escucha,
Joven y hermoso, como dios nimbado
Por esa gracia pura e intocable del mancebo,
Existiendo en el sueño imposible de una vida
Que queda sólo en música y que es como música,
Fundido con el mito al contemplarlo, forma ya de ese mito
De pureza rebelde que tierra apenas toca
Del éter huésped desterrado. La melodía le ayuda a conocerse,
A enamorarse de lo que él mismo es. Y para siempre en la música vive.

In the other's life his own finds certitude.
Love alone provides the king a reason to be alive,
His impotence forgotten, desire gratified
All through his being that suffered so long.
He leans back and regards himself in the current
Of melody and, his image set apart, awaits his remedy
In the upheaval he's feeling deep inside himself.
Isn't it enough that his love exists, out there?
To contemplate the beautiful, isn't that enough?

The gods were listening, and fulfill his desire
(So the gods punish by giving men
What they ask for), and the king's destiny,
Desiring himself, transforms him,
As into a flower, a beautiful thing, defenseless, ineffective,
Until his life ends being governed by lackeys
Yet having on them, in dying, a king's revenge.
The shadows of his dreams were for him the truth of life.
He belonged to no one, and could call no one his.

The king is there now, in his box, and he listens alone,
Beautiful and young, like a god afloat
In that pure untouchable grace of the young man,
Existing in the impossible dream of a life
That abides in music alone and is like music,
Made one with the myth by witnessing it, now a form of that myth
Of rebellious purity that scarcely touches the earth,
An exiled guest of the ether. The melody enables him to know himself,
To fall in love with who he truly is. And in the music he lives forever.

J. R. J. contempla el crepúsculo

"Señor, el crepúsculo", anunciaba
Puntual a la tarde la doncella
Entrando en el salón de Mr. Ruskin,
Algún tiempo después de consumido
El té. Y entonces Mr. Ruskin
Iba al jardín.

J. R. Jr. Contemplates the Twilight

"Sir, the twilight," the maid
Announced, entering Mr. Ruskin's parlor
Punctually just as night was falling,
A while after he had finished
Tea. And then Mr. Ruskin
Went out into the garden.

A J. R. J.

La doncella no anunciaba el crepúsculo
Ni poseía jardín donde observarlo.
Mas iba a los cristales
De su balcón y, corrido el visillo,
Desde allí contemplaba.

El crepúsculo nórdico, lento, exige
A su contemplador una atención asidua,
Velando nuestro fuego originario
(Para Heráclito la sustancia primera),
En su proceso, con celajes y visos
Delicados, cambiantes.

Al fin el ave fabulosa
Partía al hemisferio
Sombroso ahora, tras de sí dejando
De su retorno una costumbre.
Y la noche ancestral le sucedía
No contemplada ya por J. R. J.

To J. R. Jr.

The maid did not announce the twilight
Nor did he have a garden from which to observe it.
But he went to the windows
Of his balcony and, pulling back the curtains,
Looked out at it from there.

The northern twilight, slow as it is, demands
Of its viewer a diligent attention,
Veiling our primal fire
(For Heraclitus the essential substance)
In its process, with streaks of clouds
And delicate, changing colors.

Finally the fabulous bird
Divided the hemisphere
Now in shadow, leaving behind
Its customary habit of return.
Followed by the ancestral night
Yet to be contemplated by J. R. Jr.

Ninfa y Pastor, *por Ticiano*

Lo que mueve al santo,
La renuncia del santo
(Niega tus deseos
Y hallarás entonces
Lo que tu corazón desea),
Son sobrehumanos. Ahí te inclinas, y pasas.
Porque algunos nacieron para santos
Y otros para ser hombres.

Acaso cerca de dejar la vida,
De nada arrepentido y siempre enamorado,
Y con pasión que no desmienta a la primera,
Quisieras, como aquel pintor viejo,
Una vez más representar la forma humana,
Hablando silencioso con ciencia ya admirable.

El cuadro aquel aún miras,
Ya no en su realidad, en la memoria;
La ninfa desnuda y reclinada
Y a su lado el pastor, absorto todo
De carnal hermosura.
El fondo neutro, insinuado
Por el pincel apenas.

Nymph and Shepherd, *by Titian*

What moves the saint,
The saint's restraint
(Renouncing your desires
You will then find
What your heart desires),
Are superhuman. You tend in that direction
But keep going. Because some were born to be saints
And others, men.

Perhaps as you approach the end of life,
Repenting nothing and always falling in love,
And with a fervor that doesn't belie what you felt at first,
You'd like, as that old painter did,
To render the human form just one more time,
Speaking through silence with deep understanding.

You can still picture that painting,
Not in reality now, but memory;
The naked nymph reclining
And at her side the shepherd, everything
Bathed in carnal beauty.
A neutral background, barely
Suggested by the brush.

La luz entera mana
Del cuerpo de la ninfa, que es el centro
Del lienzo, su razón y su gozo;
La huella creadora fresca en él todavía,
La huella de los dedos enamorados
Que, bajo su caricia, lo animaran
Con candor animal y con gracia terrestre.

Desnuda y reclinada, contemplemos
Esa curva adorable, base de la espalda,
Donde el pintor se demoró, usando con ternura
Diestra, no el pincel, mas los dedos,
Con ahínco de amor y de trabajo
Que son un acto solo, la cifra de una vida
Perfecta al acabar, igual que el sol a veces
Demora su esplendor cercano del ocaso.

Y cuánto había amado, había vivido,
Había pintado cuando pintó ese cuerpo:
Cerca de los cien años prodigiosos;
Mas su fervor humano, agradecido al mundo,
Inocente aún era en él, como en el mozo
Destinado a ser hombre sólo y para siempre.

All light flows
From the nymph's body, which is the center
Of the canvas, its reason and its pleasure;
Creation's trace still fresh in it,
The mark of enamored fingers
Caressing it to life
With animal honesty and earthy grace.

Consider that lovely curve
Of her lower back as she lies there naked,
Where the artist lingered, tenderly,
Skillfully using not the brush but his fingers,
With the passion of love and of work
In a single act, the sign of a life
Perfected at the end, just as the sun sometimes
Lingers in the splendor of going down.

The sum of what he'd loved, of what he'd lived,
He put into the painting of that body;
Close to a hundred prodigious years old;
Yet his human ardor, grateful to the world,
Kept alive the innocence in him, as in the youth
Destined forever to be nothing more than a man.

Tres misterios gozosos

El cantar de los pájaros, al alba,
      Cuando el tiempo es mas tibio,
Alegres de vivir, ya se desliza
      Entre el sueño, y de gozo
Contagia a quien despierta al nuevo día.

Alegre sonriendo a su juguete
      Pobre y roto, en la puerta
De la casa juega solo el niñito
      Consigo y, en dichosa
Ignorancia, goza de hallarse vivo.

El poeta, sobre el papel soñando
      Su poema inconcluso,
Hermoso le parece, goza y piensa
      Con razón y locura
Que nada importa: existe su poema.

Three Delicious Mysteries

The singing of birds, at dawn,
  When the weather's cooler,
Happy to be alive, it slips
  Into your sleep and infects
With pleasure the one waking to the new day.

Happily smiling at its poor
  Broken toy, the little boy plays
With it alone in the doorway
  Of his house and, blissfully
Ignorant, delights in finding himself alive.

The poet, dreaming on paper
  His unfinished poem,
It looks good to him, he's pleased and thinks
  Rightly and madly
That nothing else matters: his poem exists.

Desolación de la Quimera

Todo el ardor del día, acumulado
En asfixiante vaho, el arenal despide.
Sobre el azul tan claro de la noche
Contrasta, como imposible gotear de un agua,
El helado fulgor de las estrellas,
Orgulloso cortejo junto a la nueva luna
Que, alta ya, desdeñosa ilumina
Restos de bestias en medio de un osario.
En la distancia aúllan los chacales.

No hay agua, fronda, matorral ni césped.
En su lleno esplendor mira la luna
A la Quimera lamentable, piedra corroída
En su desierto. Como muñón, deshecha el ala;
Los pechos y las garras el tiempo ha mutilado;
Hueco de la nariz desvanecida y cabellera,
En un tiempo anillada, albergue son ahora
De las aves obscenas que se nutren
En la desolación, la muerte.

Cuando la luz lunar alcanza
A la Quimera, animarse parece en un sollozo,
Una queja que viene, no de la ruina,
De los siglos en ella enraizados, inmortales
Llorando, el no poder morir, como mueren las formas
Que el hombre procreara. Morir es duro,
Mas no poder morir, si todo muere,
Es más duro quizá. La Quimera susurra hacia la luna
Y tan dulce es su voz que a la desolación alivia.

Desolation of the Chimera

The whole day's heat, distilled
Into a suffocating vapor, the sand releases.
Against the deep blue background of the night
Like an impossible drizzle of water,
The frozen splendor of the stars
Is proudly aligned alongside the full moon
Which, from a great height, disdainfully illumines
The remains of beasts in a boneyard.
Jackals can be heard howling in the distance.

There is no water, palm frond, underbrush or pond.
In its full splendor the moon looks down
On the pitiful Chimera, its stone corroded,
In its desert. Its missing wings, like stumps;
Its breasts and claws mutilated by time;
The hollows where its vanished nose and hair
Once curled are now home
To the obscene birds feeding
On desolation, on death.

When moonlight touches
The Chimera, it seems to come alive with a sob,
A moan that rises not from the ruin
But from the centuries rooted inside it, immortally
Crying over not being able to die, as the forms
That man gives life to always die. Dying is hard,
But not being able to die, if everything dies,
Is perhaps harder still. The Chimera murmurs at the moon
And its voice is so sweet it eases its desolation.

"Sin víctimas ni amantes. ¿Donde fueron los hombres?
Ya no creen en mí, y los enigmas que yo les propusiera
Insolubles, como la Esfinge, mi rival y hermana,
Ya no les tientan. Lo divino subsiste,
Proteico y multiforme, aunque mueran los dioses.
Por eso vive en mí este afán que no pasa,
Aunque pasó mi forma, aunque ni sombra soy;
Afán que se concreta en ver rendido al hombre
Temeroso ante mí, ante mi tentador secreto indescifrable.

"Como animal domado por el látigo,
El hombre. Pero, qué hermoso; su fuerza y su hermosura,
Oh dioses, cuán cautivadoras. Delicia hay en el hombre;
Cuando el hombre es hermoso, en él cuánta delicia.
Siglos pasaron ya desde que desertara el hombre
De mí y a mis secretos desdeñoso olvidara.
Y bien que algunos pocos a mí acudan,
Los poetas, ningún encanto encuentro en ellos,
Cuando apenas les tienta mi secreto ni en ellos veo hermosura.

"Flacos o flácidos, sin cabellos, con lentes,
Desdentados. Ésa es la parte física
En mi tardío servidor; y, semejante a ella,
Su carácter. Aun así, no muchos buscan mi secreto hoy,
Que en la mujer encuentran su personal triste Quimera.
Y bien está ese olvido, porque ante mí no acudan
Tras de cambiar pañales al infante
O enjugarle nariz, mientras meditan
Reproche o alabanza de algún crítico.

"No victims, no lovers. Where did the people go?
They no longer believe in me, and the unanswerable riddles
I posed, like the Sphinx, my rival and sister,
No longer tempt them. The divine survives,
In all its protean forms, even though the gods die.
That's why this deathless desire is alive in me,
Though my form is wasted, though I'm less than a shade;
A desire to see humanity humbled
In fear before me, before my tempting indecipherable secret.

"Man is like an animal tamed
By the whip. But how beautiful; his strength and his beauty,
Oh gods, how captivating. There is delight in man;
When man is beautiful, how delightful he is.
Centuries have passed since man deserted
Me and disdainfully forgot my secrets.
And while a few still pay me some attention,
I find no enchantment among the poets,
As my secret scarcely tempts them and I see in them no beauty.

"Skinny, flaccid, balding, bespectacled,
Toothless. That's the physical aspect
Of my former servant; and his character
Looks the same. Even so, not many seek my secret now,
Since they find in woman their personal sad Chimera.
And it's just as well I'm forgotten, because anyone
Changing infants' diapers and wiping noses while he thinks
About some critic's praise or bad review
Has no time to pay me any attention.

"¿Es que pueden creer en ser poetas
Si ya no tienen el poder, la locura
Para creer en mí y en mi secreto?
Mejor les va sillón en academia
Que la aridez, la ruina y la muerte,
Recompensas que generosa di a mis víctimas,
Una vez ya tomada posesión de sus almas,
Cuando el hombre y el poeta preferían
Un miraje cruel a certeza burguesa.

"Bien otros fueron para mí los tiempos
Cuando feliz, ligera, hollaba el laberinto
Donde a tantos perdí y a tantos otros los dotaba
De mi eterna locura: imaginar dichoso, sueños de futuro,
Esperanzas de amor, periplos soleados.
Mas, si prudente, estrangulaba al hombre
Con mis garras potentes, que un grano de locura
Sal de la vida es. A fuerza de haber sido,
Promesas para el hombre ya no tengo."

Su reflejo la luna deslizando
Sobre la arena sorda del desierto,
Entre sombras a la Quimera deja,
Calla en su dulce voz la música cautiva.
Y como el mar en la resaca, al retirarse
Deja a la playa desnuda de su magia,
Retirado el encanto de la voz, queda el desierto
Todavía más inhóspito, sus dunas
Ciegas y opacas, sin el miraje antiguo.

"Can they really believe in being poets
If they no longer have the power, the madness
To believe in me and my secret?
Better for them an academic chair
Than barrenness, ruin and death,
The generous recompense I gave my victims,
Once I had possession of their souls,
When men and poets still preferred
A cruel mirage to bourgeois certainty.

"Clearly for me those times were different
When with a light heart I danced happily through the labyrinth
Where I lost so many and so many others I endowed
With my eternal madness: joyful imagination, dreams of the future,
Hopes of love, sunny voyages.
But the prudent ones, the cautious men, I strangled
With my powerful claws, since a grain of madness
Is the salt of life. Now that I've been and gone,
I don't have any more promises for man."

The moon's reflection sliding
Over the deaf sand of the desert
Leaves the Chimera stranded among shadows,
The captive music of its sweet voice quieted.
And as the sea pulls back the tide
Leaving the beach denuded of its magic,
The voice's spell, pulled back, leaves the desert
Even more unwelcoming, its dunes
Blind, dulled without the old mirage.

Muda y en sombra, parece la Quimera retraerse
A la noche ancestral del Caos primero;
Mas ni dioses, ni hombres, ni sus obras,
Se anulan si una vez son; existir deben
Hasta el amargo fin, perdiéndose en el polvo.
Inmóvil, triste, la Quimera sin nariz olfatea
Frescor de alba naciente, alba de otra jornada
Que no habrá de traerle piadosa la muerte,
Sino que su existir desolado prolongue todavía.

Mute, in darkness, the Chimera seems to have retreated
Into the ancestral night of primal Chaos;
But neither gods, nor men, nor their creations
Are ever nullified once they've been; they must exist
Until the bitter end, disappearing into the dust.
Immobile, sad, the noseless Chimera can smell
The freshness of dawn, dawn of another day
When death will not have pity on it,
But its desolate existence will continue.

Amigos: Enrique Asúnsolo

Me iba por tiempo no más largo
Del que, entre una y otra visita, distanciaba,
Por su poca salud, la ocasión de vernos
Y, al despedirme, dijo: "Quizá cuando regrese
Ya no me encuentre." No le creía. Pero, ¿cómo ayudarle
Ante el final que afrontaremos solos?

Ausente yo, brusca y definitiva, la noticia
De su muerte. Y recordé: ante alguna bebida
Bien compuesta, ante algún plato
Bien ordenado, con él, de humor sutil, aquellas horas
Que, al pasar, no dejaban saciedad ni fastidio,
Cuando yo estaba, por una vez, en compañía.

Acaso no sea justo al decir sólo eso:
Poesía y pintura (hizo de mí un retrato),
Aficiones en él gemelas, tácito fondo eran,
Dándole otro valor a la amistad que nos unía.
Pero saber vivir fue su don más profundo.

Quisiera verle aún. ¿De qué muerto podemos decir eso?
Oída su palabra, todo cansa: lugar, cosa, persona.
Mas él, al irse, tras de sí deja viva la apetencia
De la conversación y la amistad interrumpidas.

Friends: Enrique Asúnsolo

I was going away for a time no longer
Than the usual breaks we took,
Because of his bad health, between our meetings,
And as I was saying goodbye he said: "Maybe when you come back
You won't find me here." I didn't believe him. But how could I have helped him
Up against the end we face alone?

While I was gone, news of his death came,
Blunt and definitive. And I remembered:
Over some well mixed drink, or some well prepared
Meal, being with him, his subtle wit, those hours
Going by not sated but not bored,
When for a while I was in good company.

Maybe it isn't fair to say just that:
His twin passions, poetry and painting
(He did a portrait of me), were the tacit background,
Giving another dimension to our friendship.
But knowing how to live was his deepest gift.

I'd like to see him again. Which of the dead
Can we say that about? His talk once heard,
Everything else feels tired: places, things, people.
But leaving, he left a living appetite
For friendship and conversation interrupted.

Málibu

Málibu,
Olas con lluvia.
Aire de música.

Málibu,
Agua cautiva.
Gruta marina.

Málibu,
Nombre de hada.
Fuerza encantada.

Málibu,
Viento que ulula.
Bosque de brujas.

Málibu,
Una palabra,
Y en ella, magia.

Malibu

Malibu,
Waves in the rain.
Musical air.

Malibu,
Water contained.
Cove of the sea.

Malibu,
Fairytale name.
Enchanted force.

Malibu,
Owl-calling wind.
Wood full of witches.

Malibu,
Merely a word,
And magic in it.

Clearwater

Píntalo. Con un pincel delgado,
Con color bien ligero. Pinta
El reflejo del sol sobre las aguas,
En su fondo piedrecillas que sueñan.

Las hojas en los olmos, que algún aire,
Al orear, mansamente remueve.
Al fondo, sombra azul de unas colinas.
Quieta en el cielo, alguna nube clara.

Dentro de ti sonríe lo que esperas
Sin prisa, para su día cierto;
Espera donde feliz se refleja tu vida
Igual que este paisaje en dulces aguas.

Clearwater

Paint it. With a fine brush,
In a nice light shade. Paint
The sun glittering on the water,
Little rocks dreaming in the background.

The leaves of the elms, which a slight breeze,
Whispering, gently rustles.
Beyond, some shadowy blue hills,
Hanging in the sky, a white cloud.

Inside you smiles what you're waiting for,
In no rush, in its good time;
You wait for the place where your life is reflected
Gladly as in this freshwater landscape.

Tiempo de vivir, tiempo de dormir

Ya es noche. Vas a la ventana.
El jardín está oscuro abajo.
Ves el lucero de la tarde
Latiendo en fulgor solitario.

Y quietamente te detienes.
Dentro de ti algo se queja:
Esa hermosura no atendida
Te seduce y reclama afuera.

Encanto de estar vivo, el hombre
Sólo siente en raros momentos
Y aún necesita compartirlos
Para aprender la sombra, el sueño.

Time to Live, Time to Sleep

It's night. You go to the window.
The garden below is dark.
You see the evening star
Pulsing in lonely splendor.

And quietly you pause.
Inside you something groans:
That unattended beauty
Seduces you, calls you out.

Man only feels the enchantment
Of being alive in rare moments
And still he needs to share them
To understand darkness and dreams.

Respuesta

Lo cretino, en ti,
No excluye lo ruin.

Lo ruin, en tu sino,
No excluye lo cretino.

Así que eres, en fin,
Tan cretino como ruin.

Reply

The cretinous in you
Doesn't exclude the contemptible.

The contemptible, in your fate,
Includes the cretinous.

And so you are, in the end,
Both cretinous and contemptible.

Luna llena en semana santa

Denso, suave el aire
Orea tantas callejas,
Plazuelas, cuya alma
Es la flor del naranjo.

Resuenan cerca, lejos,
Clarines masculinos
Aquí, allí la flauta
Y oboe femeninos.

Mágica por el cielo
La luna fulge, llena
Luna de parasceve.
Azahar, luna, música,

Entrelazados, bañan
La ciudad toda. Y breve
Tu mente la contiene
En sí, como una mano

Amorosa. ¿Nostalgias?
No. Lo que así recreas
Es el tiempo sin tiempo
Del niño, los instintos

Aprendiendo la vida
Dichosamente, como
La planta nueva aprende
En suelo amigo. Eco

Full Moon During Holy Week

Rich and soft, the air
Refreshes the narrow streets,
The little plazas, whose soul
Is the orange blossom.

Near and far you can hear
Masculine clarions
Here, feminine flutes
And oboes over there.

A magic moon shines
In the sky, full
Moon of Good Friday.
Orange blossom, music, moon,

Intertwined, are bathing
The whole city. And briefly
Your mind can hold it
All, like a lover's

Hand. Nostalgia?
No. What you're reviving
Is the timeless time
Of a child, his instincts

Learning life
Happily, as
The young plant learns
In friendly soil. An echo

Que, a la doble distancia,
Generoso hoy te vuelve,
En leyenda, a tu origen.
Et in Arcadia ego.

Which, doubly distant,
Generously takes you back,
In legend, to your beginning.
Et in Arcadia ego.

El amor todavía

¿Es ésta la faz, la figura
Que entrevía tu deseo
Levantándose en tu camino,
Dominante, como tu dueño?

¿Dominante? Con inconsciencia
De un deseo loco y tardío,
Pero ofreciendo inútilmente,
Con su existencia, tu motivo.

Como el adivino en la arena
La visión halla del futuro,
En estos aires que aún extrañas
Crees hallar a tu vida un rumbo.

Rumbo prohibido, imposible,
Otra vez el viejo tormento.
Tienes opuestas las estrellas,
Opuesto está su pensamiento.

Tu vida además sólo cuenta
Con hoy apenas, no mañana.
Su juventud es triunfante,
Tu vejez al espejo habla.

La paradoja lamentable
A su regla otra vez te pliega:
Conocer lo que no conoce,
Desear lo que no desea.

Love Again

Is this the face, the form
Glimpsed by your desire
That owns you, dominant,
Setting you on your path?

Dominant? Unconscious
As a crazy, late desire,
Its existence pointlessly
Offering a reason for being.

As the fortune teller finds
In the sand the future's vision,
You think your life will find its way
In this air you're still a stranger to.

A forbidden, impossible course,
The same old torment again.
The very stars oppose it,
Their thought opposed to it.

Besides, your life counts only
And barely for today, not tomorrow.
His youth is triumphant,
Your age speaks in the mirror.

The sorry paradox again
Bends you to its rule:
To know what doesn't know,
To desire what doesn't desire.

Veneno y triaca es a un tiempo
El antiguo encanto insidioso:
En el cuerpo que tu amor crea
Aún esperas nutrir tus ojos.

The old insidious spell
Is at once poison and cure:
You still hope to feast your eyes
On the body that forms your love.

Lo que al amor le basta

De nuevo el amor tiene
Presa en ti. De servirle
A pesar de ti mismo
La edad aún no te exime.

Sin amor, libre eras,
Cuando tus ojos vieron
La nueva criatura
Que despertó al deseo.

Los ojos ya alimentan
Ese encanto en el alma
Y otra cosa no quieres.
¿Sólo contemplar basta?

¿Eso te basta? Y cómo,
Viéndola, a todo llena
Una razón; y es todo
Sin razón, al no verla.

Mirar a lo que amas.
Si bastara ese encanto
Nada más; si bastara
Este mirar lo amado.

En la fase primera
Del amor te demoras
Sin allegarte al cuerpo
Cuyo existir adoras.

What's Enough for Love

Again you've been caught
By love. Even age
Doesn't exempt you from it
In spite of yourself.

Loveless, you were free,
When your eyes beheld
The new creature
Who sparked your desire.

Your eyes still feed
That spell in your soul
And you want nothing else.
Is it enough just to see?

Is that enough for you?
Just seeing him, one thought
Fills everything; without
Seeing him, nothing makes sense.

To gaze on the one you love.
If only that spell were enough
And nothing more; if only to look
At the one you love were enough.

In the first phase
Of love you defer
Getting close to the body
Whose being you adore.

Hablando a Manona

Manonita, Manona,
Ahora has aprendido
Cómo el aire, de pronto,
Se lleva los amigos.
Y así
Tú estás ahí,
Yo estoy aquí.

A veces Dios nos hace
De un cariño regalo,
Por un poco de tiempo,
Cuando bien nos portamos.
Y al fin
Tenemos que vivir
Tú ahí, yo aquí.

¿Está bien, te parece,
Manona, Manonita,
Que el cariño no sea
Para toda la vida?
¿Y así
Tú estés ahí
Y esté yo aquí?

Speaking to Manona

Manonita, Manona,
Now you know
How the air all of a sudden
Carries away your friends.
And so
You're there
And I'm here.

Sometimes when we've been
Good, God gives us
A tender gift
For a brief time.
And in the end
We go on living,
You there, me here.

You think it's fair,
Manona, Manonita,
That tenderness can't last
A whole life long?
And that's why
You're there
And I'm here?

Esperemos, Manona;
Manonita, paciencia:
Tal vez nuestros afectos
Dios los pone a esa prueba.
Y así
Tú estás ahí
Yo estoy aquí.

Y luego una mañana,
Despertando, hallaremos
Sonrientes las caras
De los que estaban lejos.
Y al fin
No estaremos así:
Tú ahí, yo aquí.

We have to wait, Manona;
Manonita, be patient:
Maybe God is putting
Our tenderness to a test.
And that's why
You're there
And I'm here.

And then one morning
On waking we'll find
The smiling faces
Of the faraway ones.
And at last
We won't be like this:
You there, me here.

Peregrino

¿Volver? Vuelva el que tenga,
Tras largos años, tras un largo viaje,
Cansancio del camino y la codicia
De su tierra, su casa, sus amigos,
Del amor que al regreso fiel le espere.

Mas ¿tú? ¿volver? Regresar no piensas,
Sino seguir libre adelante,
Disponible por siempre, mozo o viejo,
Sin hijo que te busque, como a Ulises,
Sin Ítaca que aguarde y sin Penélope.

Sigue, sigue adelante y no regreses,
Fiel hasta el fin del camino y tu vida,
No eches de menos un destino más fácil,
Tus pies sobre la tierra antes no hollada,
Tus ojos frente a lo antes nunca visto.

Pilgrim

Go back? He may go back who has,
After long years, after a long journey,
Grown weary of the road and longs
For his land, his house, his friends,
The love faithfully awaiting his return.

But you? Go back? You don't think of going back,
But going on freely ahead,
Young or old, ready for anything,
Without a son to seek you, like Ulysses,
Without an Ithaca waiting and without Penelope.

Go on, go on ahead and don't look back,
Faithful until the end to the road, your life,
Don't wish you had an easier destiny,
Your feet on ground that's never been walked before,
Your eyes wide to what hasn't yet been seen.

Dos de noviembre

Las campanas hoy
Ominosas suenan.
Aún temprano, el aire,
Frío acero, llega

Por tu sangre adentro.
Recuerdas los tuyos
Idos este año
Dejándote único.

Ahora tú sostienes
Solo la memoria:
El hogar remoto,
Familiares sombras,

Todo destinado
Contigo al olvido.
El azul del cielo
Promete, tan limpio,

Aire tibio luego.
Y por el mercado,
Donde están las flores
En copiosos ramos,

Un olor respiras,
Olor, mas no aroma,
A tierra, a hermosura
Que, antigua, conforta.

November Second

The bells today
Sound ominous.
Even early, the cold
Steel air comes

Into your blood.
You recall your own,
Gone this year,
Leaving you alone.

Now you have
Only memory:
The faraway home,
Shadows of family,

Everything destined
With you for oblivion.
The sky's clear
Blue promises

Warm air later.
And in the market,
Where bunches of
Flowers abound,

You breathe a smell,
A smell, not an aroma,
Of earth, of beauty,
Ancient and comforting.

A pesar del tiempo,
Al alma, en la vida,
Materia y sentidos
Como siempre alivian.

In spite of time,
As always in life
Things and the senses
Lighten the soul.

1936

Recuérdalo tú y recuérdalo a otros,
Cuando asqueados de la bajeza humana,
Cuando iracundos de la dureza humana:
Este hombre solo, este acto solo, esta fe sola.
Recuérdalo tú y recuérdalo a otros.

En 1961 y en ciudad extraña,
Más de un cuarto de siglo
Después. Trivial la circunstancia,
Forzado tú a pública lectura,
Por ella con aquel hombre conversaste:
Un antiguo soldado
En la Brigada Lincoln.

Veinticinco años hace, este hombre,
Sin conocer tu tierra, para él lejana
Y extraña toda, escogió ir a ella
Y en ella, si la ocasión llegaba, decidió a apostar su vida,
Juzgando que la causa allá puesta al tablero
Entonces, digna era
De luchar por la fe que su vida llenaba.

Que aquella causa aparezca perdida,
Nada importa;
Que tantos otros, pretendiendo fe en ella
Sólo atendieran a ellos mismos,
Importa menos.
Lo que importa y nos basta es la fe de uno.

1936

Remember him and remember him to others,
When you're disgusted with human baseness,
When you're enraged at human coldness:
This single man, this single act, this single faith.
Remember him and remember him to others.

In 1961, in a foreign city,
More than a quarter century
Later. A trivial situation,
You were forced to give a public reading,
And so had a conversation with that man:
An old soldier
In the Lincoln Brigade.

Twenty-five years ago, this man,
Not knowing your land—to him, far away
And utterly foreign—chose to go there
And there, if need be, decided to stake his life,
Judging the cause on the line
At the time worth
Fighting for, in the faith filling his existence.

That the cause seems lost
Doesn't matter;
That so many others, pretending faith in it,
Only served themselves
Matters still less.
What counts and suffices is the faith of one.

Por eso otra vez hoy la causa te aparece
Como en aquellos días:
Noble y tan digna de luchar por ella.
Y su fe, la fe aquella, él la ha mantenido
A través de los años, la derrota,
Cuando todo parece traicionarla.
Mas esa fe, te dices, es lo que sólo importa.

Gracias, Compañero, gracias
Por el ejemplo. Gracias porque me dices
Que el hombre es noble.
Nada importa que tan pocos lo sean:
Uno, uno tan sólo basta
Como testigo irrefutable
De toda la nobleza humana.

That's why today the cause seems
As it was then:
Noble and well worth fighting for.
And his faith, that faith, he's kept alive
Over the years, across defeat,
When everything seems to betray it.
But that faith, tell yourself, is all that matters.

Thanks, Compañero, thanks
For the example. Thanks for telling me
Man is noble.
What difference does it make that so few are:
One, just one is enough—
An irrefutable witness
To human honor.

Despedida

Muchachos
Que nunca fuisteis compañeros de mi vida,
Adiós.
Muchachos
Que no seréis nunca compañeros de mi vida,
Adiós.

El tiempo de una vida nos separa
Infranqueable:
A un lado la juventud libre y risueña;
A otro la vejez humillante e inhóspita.

De joven no sabía
Ver la hermosura, codiciarla, poseerla;
De viejo la he aprendido
Y veo a la hermosura, mas la codicio inútilmente.

Mano de viejo mancha
El cuerpo juvenil si intenta acariciarlo.
Con solitaria dignidad el viejo debe
Pasar de largo junto a la tentación tardía.

Frescos y codiciables son los labios besados,
Labios nunca besados más codiciables y frescos aparecen.
¿Qué remedio, amigos? ¿Qué remedio?
Bien lo sé: no lo hay.

Taking Leave

Boys
Who never were companions in my life,
Goodbye.
Boys
Who'll never be companions in my life,
Goodbye.

A lifetime divides us
Insurmountably:
On one side youth, smiling and free;
On the other old age, desolate and pathetic.

When I was young I didn't know how
To recognize beauty, crave it, possess it;
Now that I'm old I've learned
And I can see beauty, but what's the point of craving.

The hand of an old man puts a dark mark
On any young body it tries to touch.
Alone and dignified an old man ought
To steer well clear of those last temptations.

Fresh and desirable are the lips you've kissed,
Fresher and sweeter still the ones you've never kissed.
What can you do, friends? What can you do?
I know, I know: not a thing.

Qué dulce hubiera sido
En vuestra compañía vivir un tiempo:
Bañarse juntos en aguas de una playa caliente,
Compartir bebida y alimento en una mesa.
Sonreír, conversar, pasearse
Mirando cerca, en vuestros ojos, esa luz y esa música.

Seguid, seguid así, tan descuidadamente,
Atrayendo al amor, atrayendo al deseo.
No cuidéis de la herida que la hermosura vuestra y vuestra gracia abren
En este transeúnte inmune en apariencia a ellas.

Adiós, adiós, manojos de gracias y donaires.
Que yo pronto he de irme, confiado,
Adonde, anudado el roto hilo, diga y haga
Lo que aquí falta, lo que a tiempo decir y hacer aquí no supe.

Adiós, adiós, compañeros imposibles.
Que ya tan sólo aprendo
A morir, deseando
Veros de nuevo, hermosos igualmente
En alguna otra vida.

How tender it might have been
To live once in your company:
Go swimming together in the surf of a hot beach,
Eat and drink together around a table,
Smile, talk, walk around town
Seeing that light, that music deep in your eyes.

Go on, go on like that, so recklessly,
Stirring up love, stirring up desire.
Ignore the wound you open with your beauty and your grace
In this wanderer seemingly immune to them.

Goodbye, goodbye, handfuls of grace and charm.
I'll soon be on my way, it's a sure thing,
To where the broken thread's retied and what's missing here,
What I never knew how to say and do here at the time,
Will be said and done.

Goodbye, goodbye, impossible companions.
Now all that's left for me to learn is how
To die, longing
To see you again, as lovely as ever,
In some other life.

Notes on the Poems

"Eagle and Rose," page 45. This is Cernuda's highly subjective revisionist account of the ill-starred marriage of Philip II of Spain and Mary I of England, which lasted from 1554 to her death in 1558. The poet, who had spent nearly ten years of his exile in Great Britain, implicitly identifies with both the proud Spanish monarch in a less than hospitable land and the barren queen destined to die childless.

"With Regard to Flowers," page 133. The "young poet" is John Keats. I've been unable to find the quoted "final words" Cernuda cites in Spanish, so have omitted quotes in the translation.

"Once More, with Feeling," page 139. The poem refers to García Lorca and his posthumous "appropriation" and mythification.

"Louis of Bavaria Listens to Lohengrin," page 147. Louis II (commonly known in German as Ludwig, but Cernuda uses the Spanish equivalent Luis, no doubt as an echo of his own name) was king of Bavaria from 1864 to 1886. A friend and patron of Richard Wagner, he was known to be "eccentric" and eventually deemed insane and confined to his chateau on Lake Starnberg where he committed suicide by drowning. Cernuda reimagines him here as an avatar of the Narcissus myth.

"J. R. Jr. Contemplates the Twilight," page 155, and "To J. R. Jr.," page 157. The initials "J. R. J." in the original titles of these poems would evoke for any Spaniard the figure of Juan Ramón Jiménez, but Cernuda here appears to be teasing his countrymen by specifically invoking the English writer John Ruskin, whose initials match those of the Nobel laureate (1956) and Spanish master Jiménez. Ruskin's estheticism, his elegant prose style, his ambiguous sexuality and his eventual mental instability could easily have resonated with Cernuda's sense of his own alienation. Jiménez, at the pinnacle of Spanish culture and the end of his life when this poem was written, can be seen in this context as a cruelly ironic counterpoint.

"Desolation of the Chimera," page 165. In Greek myth, the Chimera is a monster with a lion's head, a goat's body and a serpent's tail. In Cernuda's poem we find this figure embodied in a sculptural ruin set in a wasteland lamenting the irrelevance of its former power. Compare Shelley's sonnet "Ozymandias."

A Note on the Author

One of Spain's leading twentieth-century poets, Luis Cernuda was born in Seville in 1902 and came of age in Madrid among the Generation of 1927 (Alberti, Aleixandre, García Lorca, Guillén, Salinas, et al.). Two years into the Spanish Civil War, in 1938, he left Spain to lecture in England and never returned. He taught in London and in Glasgow, Scotland, until 1947 when he accepted an offer to teach at Mount Holyoke College in Massachusetts. From there he moved to Mexico in 1952, and except for brief teaching jobs in the early 1960s at UCLA and San Francisco State, he remained in Mexico until his sudden death from a heart attack in 1963. Cernuda is today considered by many in Spain to be the most influential poet of his generation. His alienation, cosmopolitanism, open homosexuality and independence of thought—he was also a prolific critic—have resonated with generations of Spanish writers and intellectuals coming to maturity since the death of dictator Francisco Franco in 1975. Cernuda's previous books in English include a *Selected Poems,* translated by Reginald Gibbons, and his collected prose poems, *Written in Water,* translated by Stephen Kessler, which received a 2004 Lambda Literary Award.

A Note on the Translator

Stephen Kessler is a poet, translator, essayist and editor whose previous translations include *Save Twilight*, selected poems of Julio Cortázar; *Eyeseas*, poems by Raymond Queneau (co-translated with Daniela Hurezanu); *Destruction or Love*, poems by Vicente Aleixandre; *Aphorisms*, prose by César Vallejo; *The Funhouse*, a novel by Fernando Alegría; and a new version of Pablo Neruda's "Alturas de Machu Picchu" in *Machu Picchu*, a book of photographs by Barry Brukoff, among other books. His most recent books of original poetry include *Burning Daylight*, *Tell It to the Rabbis* and *After Modigliani*. He is also the author of a collection of essays, *Moving Targets: On Poets, Poetry & Translation*. He lives in Northern California where he edits *The Redwood Coast Review*. For more about Stephen Kessler, visit www.stephenkessler.com.